Make Better Bets

Make Better Bets

First Edition

Jack Allweil

ISBN 978-1-7348956-1-2

All the charts were produced in Microsoft Excel and special thanks for early reading and editing goes to my mom, Catherine Brown.

To Elena Fazilova, my family, and Professor Stefan Szymanski for supporting me and getting me going. I hope this book can do the same for someone else.

Prologue

I want to describe a story. Not really a story but more of an obsession. Some may obsess over sex, drugs, and rock and roll. And while I like some or all of those my obsession, or better stated addiction, is soccer. Now I don't want to be overly dramatic but while some of you will hear the word soccer and instantly not purchase my book I ask you something that hopefully will spark your interest. Have you ever had something in your life that made you thankful to live, thankful to be here on this earth? Maybe you have and I would say you are a lucky one. I challenge you to keep an open mind and continue exploring opportunities to reach that level. While soccer is a big help in my life I'm still working to get to that level. I hope this story may help someone believe that sometimes the lowest points of one's life are truly the most special, revealing, and galvanizing of any moments on this planet.

Part I

Get Dat Money

I moseyed into the spacious Bank of America building in Wilmington, Delaware still in my early flight hoody. You see the hoody would help me keep the cash safe while going back to my car, duh, and in doing so be incredibly stylish on this slightly dreary June day. Today I was moving with purpose and zest, and quietly chuckled to the bank lady, "I have a fairly sizable withdrawal to make."

She seemed to preemptively discount any amount that she thought I would tell her, her eyes scanning me up and down, "how big are we talking?"

"Eight thousand." The other contributors of money, mostly my dad and brother, had decided to tone down their bets when I talked of issues I was having with the online gambling site, Bovada, and the fact that I'd have to take this out in cash now. I was putting in six thousand dollars of my own hard-earned money. She scanned me up and down and was clearly taken aback.

She quietly replied, "Ok. I'm the only one here but I'll see what I can do." I was not sure what that meant but... "oy, is it ok that the last two thousand are in twenties?" She seemed twitchy. Once again, not sure why.

"Yeah, that's fine." I saw her reaching into her drawer. Why are you nervous? I'm the one who's about to walk down this unknown street with eight thousand dollars in my pockets and hopefully not get mugged in the process. All you do is send that money through that little counting machine and hand it to me, no big deal. I realized I had never held that much money at one time and it was slightly odd to see that all those work hours actually generated something. All those aching hours sitting in my cubicle pondering what it was I should be doing with my life. All those hours studying for actuarial exams in tiny solo rooms, tucked in the basements of various universities, spanning multiple regions of the country and life stages, made for a lonely existence. That painful isolation that led me almost to tears on multiple occasions and formulaically drove me to shift my mind elsewhere.

She passed me the money in two wads of cash, each having a blue band wrapped around the middle. One was slightly bigger, that must be the one with all the twenties. I saw her pass all the money through the counting machine but I still wanted to go to my car and count it. I felt on edge when I had that much in my hands. At any moment someone could punch me, take the money and I'd probably never see it again. Those thoughts never had gone through my head before. Now those things were the only thing occupying my mind. It is funny what money does. I wonder how Pablo Escobar felt; I had just eight thousand.

My hoodie was over my head, hands in my kangaroo pouch, with my tight white jean shorts clinging to my skin. The only difference between a normal day and today was there was a bump directly on top of my belly button bulging. This was something I wish I had a picture of. Better yet, I would like an aerial picture from a drone at a 45-degree angle from my eyeline, about 100 feet in the air, capturing this moment in my life. The image of me diligently walking the few deserted Wilmington blocks back to my car from the bank. Hoody up, head down, and hands in pouch. My heart was racing as I pulled the door open and then quickly shut. It felt like I was the only person on earth. Am I actually doing this?

I set my backpack in the passenger's seat and kept my head on a swivel, like a wide receiver going on a pattern over the middle, constantly scanning around my car as I had these two wads of cash in my lap. Hundy, two hundy, three hundy... The counting took some time. I lost track a couple of times. Wow. Fantastic, it's all here. Let's get out of here! On to Dover Downs with a week to spare before the 2018 FIFA World Cup in Russia.

You're Fired!

November 6th, 2016 is a day that will live with me forever. My boss called me into her office and there was a stone still HR woman, shoulder pads and all, sitting in the corner of the room with slight disappointment, and moderate sadness, on her face. I knew this wasn't warm fuzzy news. I will admit to having mentally checked out months ago, when just in a little over a year I was working under my third different boss. I would even say that after the second boss I started just going through the motions. Simply put, life at Scottish Re was tough and not going well. I was working as an associate actuary doing valuation related activities at a reinsurance company. While I'm sure you think it is truly thrilling and would pounce at the opportunity to ask me all sorts of questions I would respond with a calm, "please, cool your jets."

I was about to get fired, or I was about 99.9% sure of it. One did not need to be an actuary to figure out that percentage. After an awkward pause of my boss looking at the HR woman my boss got things rolling, "Jack, it's just not working out and you will no longer be an employee of Scottish Re. This is effective immediately. Do you have anything to say?"

I thought that was a bizarre thing to ask. Um, I'm sorry? Thank you I suppose. What was I to say to that? The only thing that was going through my head was, 'damn, if only they could have done this like a week ago I could be in north London watching my beloved Arsenal play their rivals Tottenham in one of the greatest football rivalries. And I don't mean American football. Arsenal, the Kings of London, or more commonly known as the

Gunners, were my favorite sports team on earth and the thought of football brought me, albeit only a fraction of a second, some relief.

As a youngster we did not get to watch a lot of European football matches as there was no NBC Sports tv package, that plays essentially every premier league game, like there is today. I was passively a Juventus fan growing up, a team playing in the Italian Serie A. It was more a product of me admiring Zlatan Ibrahimovic, a giant Swedish renegade that happened to be a fantastic footballer, and their black and white chic jersey design than me having a real connection to Juventus. When Juventus got hit with a match fixing scandal in 2006, I was a junior in high school at the time, Juventus was banished to Serie B and Zlatan took off to Inter Milan. I was left seeing him play only rarely and it felt wrong cheering for Inter Milan. Another thing happened in 2006 that caught my attention and didn't feel so wrong.

It was the USA's first World Cup game in Germany against the 7th ranked Czech Republic team. The Czechs had a Juventus player in Pavel Nedved who was world class but the rest of the Czechs were total unknowns to me. My buddies and I were sitting in a Buffalo Wild Wings in Bay City, Michigan excited for the first five minutes only to be deflated upon the Czechs scoring off a header. About thirty minutes later I saw a goal that would, no joke, change the trajectory of my life. This little Czech guy with long brown hair, blue Nike shoes, absolutely cranked a ball from about thirty yards out. He was on the left side of the field and the ball screamed through the air and went into the upper right corner of the goal leaving the goalkeeper zero chance of saving it. The little Czech man's reaction was one of just uncontrolled joy as he outstretched his arms to welcome the hugs of his teammates. At the time I remember thinking that was the type of player I always wanted to be. This dude was total class personified and I still feel tears coming on when I watch that play. His name was Thomas Rosicky and after that World Cup he would be transferred from Borussia Dortmund, in the German Bundesliga, to Arsenal, in the English Premier League. The rest is history.

I took a deep breath and exhaled, staring at the round table between my boss, the HR lady, and me as it was hard for me to look them in their eyes, "I have to say I feel quite relieved. I could tell something was off with me being here. Thanks for the opportunity I suppose." A few short moments later, after signing some release forms, which included a generous severance, I realized I would not be coming back here. And while I was scared some I also felt liberated.

Little did I know that this firing would set off a chain of events that would change my life forever.

Going Back to My Roots!

What's the most responsible thing one can possibly think of doing when one gets fired? Cut a bunch of stuff like NetFlix accounts and maybe some insurances you don't use? Maybe eat out less, go to the movies less and less and less and less. Perhaps, perhaps that would be "wise". Or perhaps one can take that very momentous firing and take full advantage of the newly found time to explore things that one would not normally be able to do and spend their way to enlightenment. And that, my friend, is exactly what I set out to do.

I wanted to take a trip. It was now December 2016. I wanted to clear da mind, clear da soul. I had It narrowed down to two different ideas. One was more of a beach and relaxation trip. That involved going to Australia and New Zealand. Remember this was in December. The southern hemisphere is nice and toasty during that month. For all I knew it was nice there all the time but I don't know, I've never been there! I thought about the beaches and the beaches (if you know what I mean).

The other option was a bit more of a self-reflecting trip. I was thinking of exploring Eastern Europe. My grandfather on my dad's side, who I never had the privilege of meeting, grew up in Krakow and my mom still had relatives living in Poland. I found out recently that technically Krakow was part of Austria at the time but is now, once again, part of Poland. I find this almost comical now as my girlfriend is from Austria and I joke with her that I am much more Austrian than she is as her parents are from what is now Uzbekistan and Tajikistan.

Krakow is about 40 minutes from the Auschwitz concentration camp where about a million Jews were exterminated in gas chambers. My grandfather didn't like the Poles as they were incredibly anti-Semitic and that can be a slight problem when one is Jewish. His family fled Krakow for the greater Detroit area in the mid-1910's. Grandpa Jack didn't like telling people that he was Polish.

My dad's mother's family was from Hungary. I knew very little about Hungary. I knew Budapest was one of the places where college math students at the University of Michigan would go study abroad. That was about all I knew. I never once considered going to study abroad. I was a simple Michigan boy. It turns out to be a damn shame that I never considered Budapest. Despite these two Slovak women bamboozling me in Budapest it was an incredibly enjoyable city (maybe more to come on that).

I chose the second option if I didn't just give it away. I was going to go to Poland, Hungary, and the Czech Republic and while I didn't know exactly the order or the mode of transportation those were the spots I wanted to check out.

It was this trip that introduced me to reading. And I don't mean that I couldn't read before. That's not it. What I mean is I started thinking about things and actively searching out for sources to educate myself on whatever I was curious about. Now I read a ton of books on soccer, some history, and all sorts of alternative investments.

That longing to read though came in a place no other than grandpa Jack's old stomping grounds in Krakow. It's one thing to read how many Jews died during the Holocaust from Poland, about three million. It's another thing to see so many vacant synagogues with klezmer bands playing outside, almost as a tourist attraction that Jews used to live here. This was modern day Krakow and that is what spurred my purchase of a book on the Polish – Jewish relationship. I could not put that thing down. How could this happen?

While I was in Poland it saddened me to see all the old synagogues. Old synagogues on their own sound like a cool feature or great symbol but the problem is there are so few Jews there now, and certainly not enough to fill those synagogues. It's one thing to read in a book that Poland was the country with the most Jews in the entire world. Three and a half million Jews lived in Poland! That's mind boggling to me as my siblings and myself were the only Jews in our village in Michigan, situated on Lake Huron, and the only Jews in our high school of about 1400 people. Now of those three and a half million Jews that lived in Poland three million of them were killed during the Holocaust. Hitler most likely based his plans trampolining off the anti-Semitic feelings prevalent in Poland. Now like I said it's one thing to read those figures in a book but to see all the vacant, ghost like, synagogues is a different thing and gave me the heebie geebies.

When I was a youngen I often affiliated myself mostly with my Polish heritage, as they had a decent soccer team that I passively rooted for, but after going there I felt so sad. I went to a local soccer game between Poznan and the local team, Cracovia. It was the first time I had to get my picture taken and pledge my allegiance to a team to attend a game. They were very strict on where fans from the opposing sides would sit during the game. It seemed like the fan bases were separated in the stadium but I was not quite sure how they did that as I did not see separate entrances. Soccer hooliganism seemed a modest problem in Poland as even my AirBnB host had mentioned the possibility of there being violence at the game and to watch myself.

When I was in that stadium on that crisp winter night, toes going numb in my sneakers sitting 2nd row off the field in a quarter filled stadium, I had a moment where I was thinking this could have been my life. If my grandfather would have stayed there, and I suppose many other serendipitous things happened, I could have grown up there, cheered for this team, and dreamt of playing for them. At that moment I felt utterly disgusted towards the Poles. I simply did not like them.

Despite my anger I was still trying to pick up on everything I was seeing and hearing in the stadium. The home supporters behind the goal struck me as aggressive football fans. There was constant cheering and aggressive chirping. The odd thing was that the chanting had no rhyme or reason. If a player on Cracovia was rewarded a direct kick or made a great play there was no cheering and if the referee missed a call for them there was no booing. What gives? Their chanting was loud but steady and didn't alter with anything that was happening on the field. I found this very weird. It was almost like they weren't even watching the game and were more interested in themselves chanting than their actual team that was working hard. How could they watch one of their players get knocked down with the absence of a whistle and keep chanting? A goal came and no change in the fans' demeanor. Interesting... Sounds familiar.

I was very confused at my anger towards Poland as everyone I had met in Poland up to that point had been perfectly pleasant towards me. I was anxious because I could not figure why I was feeling this. Krakow was a very unique city, filled with big buildings, slightly gothic looking, and many college kids strolling to and fro. I think I was feeling disgust because I could have grown up here! Objectively this place was very cool. It was a hipster place, with pretty girls and soccer galore. What more could one ask for? Great pizza, they had it. Great sushi, they had it. I could have been getting delicious croissants in the heart of the city, strolling alongside the lightly fogged mystic river in the morning with a big castle to my back, just like I did every morning while I was there. I could have been running along this river every morning! This could have been my life. But other parts of Krakow reminded me of how my life may have so nearly never happened.

There were reminders all around that life here would have not been so good when 1941 rolled around. There were the touristy cafes with Klezmer bands and huge Jewish cemeteries. There were signs, with the star of David, to get to Kazimierz, the Jewish section once upon a time that had morphed into a cultural and progressive part of the city. There were framed pictures of the shooting of Steven Spielberg's Schindler's List around the Jewish courtyard showing that Jews were at least ok with coming back here. Schindler's factory was just on the other side of the Vistula river, right in the heart of the Krakow Jewish ghetto. I was really understanding why the lucky ones who could leave did leave. And I figured I'd be even more reminded of that theme visiting Auschwitz the next morning.

The synagogues were just relics in Krakow and one even had a bookstore attached to it that sold books and Jewish items. It was there where I bought a book on the dynamic between the Jews and the Poles that set off a cascade of reading[1]. Once upon a time Poland had more Jews than any other country on the planet but now it was a totally different ball game.

Part II

Szymanski

After my newly found love for reading coupled with a ton of time, as I didn't have a job, I began to generate more and more ideas. I was sucked into a black hole of soccer books. It seemed after I read one I needed to read them all. Money and Soccer, Soccernomics, 12 Yards, Das Reboot, I am Zlatan, Messi, and My Turn. They were all great for their different reasons but the two that really changed some of my thinking were Soccernomics and Money and Soccer. They were written by these two guys who really analyzed the game, and the influencers behind the game, and came up with some insightful findings. Simon Kupir was more of a cultural writer and did a lot of the Dutch soccer stories including The Dutch, The War which was about the Dutch club Ajax during World War II. The other guy was Stefan Szymanski. He was an English bloak who oddly enough worked in the Kinesiology department at the University of Michigan, where I went to school, and did most of the analytics for these research projects.

Soccernomics[2] and Money and Soccer[3] are an extension of each other in my mind. They are so blended in my mind that from here on out when I say Soccernomics I could mean either Soccernomics or Money and Soccer. Soccernomics had a section where they were trying to answer the question of which country uses their resources best in soccer. I was mesmerized by the question itself and questioning how someone could measure it. I suppose I thought it's either in the culture or it's not but they made me see things a bit differently. They were looking at GDP per capita, population, and number of international appearances a country had participated in to predict the goal differential between two countries squaring off on the international stage. They were looking at countries that outdid the goal differential they were predicted by a country with their resources.

After being in Iceland with my brother in 2016 and seeing all the soccer fields it didn't really strike me as surprising that Iceland scored well in the Soccernomics analysis. With only some three hundred thousand people it was amazing they could compete with the likes of the best in Europe. The old Yugoslavian countries, like Croatia and Serbia, also scored well. I was very intrigued by this. Although they found those three factors only accounted for about 25% of the goal difference that got my mind spinning. What else might be able to help predict goal difference?

I was determined to talk to Szymanski. I called him multiple times at the university to talk to him and maybe get some insights or help. Four times I tried to call him with no pick up and no reply. I thought about throwing in the towel but called a fifth. No response. What was this guy doing? Was he so busy he really couldn't pick up my call? He was a professor, not the President of the United States. Sixth time, winner winner chicken dinner! I was actually surprised when he picked up the phone. It was almost turning into one of those times where you're calling a pretty girl and slightly hoping they don't pick up so you can just leave a message and to at least tell yourself you tried. Please don't tell me I'm alone on that sentiment.

I started telling him that I loved his book and I'm guessing he doesn't get many fan calls. Kurplop, I heard him drop his notepad or maybe even his laptop. I won't go as far as to say he sounded in shock, but I would say legitimately surprised. "Oh really?" he asked.

He was very eager to help me and oddly curious as to what I was all about. "Where are you from?" he asked.

"About 100 miles north of Detroit on Lake Huron. It's a super small town, Linwood, just north of Bay City and Saginaw, you may have heard of those. But I went to Ann Arbor for school and lived there 3 years while working as an actuary in one of the Detroit suburbs. I thought it was a cool coincidence when I saw you worked at U of M."

He replied, "oh, I'm sorry you're from there." That was a slightly dickish thing to say but I'll let it slide even though it didn't sound entirely playful. I perfectly liked where I grew up. I just got a bit tired of being so cold.

I started explaining to him what I was thinking about doing. I wanted to start looking at factors that could help me predict goal difference and in turn help predict the chances of team A beating team B. I would then look at what the Vegas odds were compared to what I was predicting and purchase the bargain picks, or at least take my chances on the bets that weren't a complete rip off. I was looking for value, maybe Portugal paying $1.80 for every $1 to win their group was a super bet, or maybe Iceland getting out of Argentina's group with getting $2.5 for every $1 bet.

"Here let me get something. I have my sources written somewhere over here."

Say what? He was going to give me his sources? Damn this was so easy! One phone call, that's all it took. Well really six phone calls are all it took.

Szymanski continued, "So I got all the game scores from a German site called laenderspiel.de but it comes in English too, think also in French. It's incredibly comprehensive. It has all the conference scores, number of international appearances, and

FIFA rankings. The country data is from the world bank database, which should have csv's going back 50 years, but you'll have to do a bit of work to break up the UK numbers to get Wales, Scotland, Northern Ireland, and England Data. So that's where we got the population and GDP/capita numbers."

I continued beginning to talk before I finished noting all of his sources, "Wow, this is so helpful. Yeah, I've done a lot of simulations and optimizations for American football and even ran a daily fantasy information site awhile but got scared they'd make it illegal, but I'm very excited to try and do something for soccer."

"So where are you now?"

"I'm working as an actuary in Charlotte, North Carolina. I've been in Charlotte about two and half years and at this job less than a year. The weather is very nice but I do miss my family a lot."

"Well, this is very cool of you to call. I'm always interested in how our data and books are received and used. I'd love to see what you end up doing with this."

"Yeah, I'll be sure to let you know. Thanks again."

And that was that. Jackie boy got dat data... Or at least the sources. Extracting the data would be an entirely different matter.

Think It Out

This was very exciting as the Russian World Cup was coming up in summer 2018. In theory this is a great idea. Do an analysis and look for value. I suppose this is the process for any business venture. If you are thinking Mexico is getting out of their group of 4 (top 2 teams in a group get out in the group stage of the World Cup) 50% of the time how much would someone need to pay you to take the bet? Well 1:1 or even money would be a "fair" bet but your risk averseness is another matter. One bets a dollar, if Mexico gets out of the group they'd get their original dollar back plus one more. If Mexico doesn't get out then the bookie keeps your dollar. You're expected collection at the end of the group stage is (probability of a win)*(collections with winning bet) + (probability of a loss)*(collections with losing bet) = .5*2 + .5*0 = 1, which is exactly what you started with. Now what if your analysis says they'll get out 50% of the time but Vegas is currently paying \$1.25 for every \$1 you bet on Mexico to get out of the World Cup group stage? Then your expected collection would be .5*(2.25) + .5*0 = 1.125 which is greater than the 1 you started with! An expected 12.5% return! This sounds like a good deal unless you're moderately risk averse and don't like to roll the dice, in which case I'm not sure if you should keep reading. Life favors the bold and pays the zaggers when others are zigging. If there's one thing I hope you takes from this book it's that line! I unfortunately can't remember who actually told me that but I've always had that thought in my head, "go zag".

Each Huge Journey Begins With One Small Step

It was November 2017 and I was sitting in my brand-new study room of my house that I just bought. It was a big house for one guy and kind of creepy if I'm being truthful. I really didn't need all that space but I've been obsessed with renting out bedrooms in a house to get the passive income. I wanted to be "Da Landlord" and I wanted to be a house hacker. It was a 4 bedroom and 3.5 bath house with 4 split levels, and even a pool in the back, which I thought ideal to rent out to potential renters. But I digress.

I was in the study room, all alone, staring at my computer on a brisk Saturday mid-morning and actually drinking coffee which I almost never do. I looked out at the covered pool and thought about all I had done to get here. All of the studying, all of the time, and all of the opportunity costs.

But I had not had a job a mere five months ago. I had been a part time Lyft and Uber driver, part time math tutor, and professional reader-eater. Seriously. I'd almost always read a book over lunch and dinner. This was quite nice, and although many would find it peculiar I would suggest getting comfortable eating alone once in a while over a book of interest. Maybe not so extreme as to eat every meal alone but you get the point. Also, you'd never believe how many people come up to talk to you if they see you reading a book alone. It's a lost art and seems to attract notice.

In the last year I had spent about a month total in Europe. I walked the streets my grandfather grew up in Krakow, marched along the abyss of Auschwitz concentration camp, met a random German girl, Ms. Kirschbaum (means cherry tree, who would have known) in Warsaw traveling back to Germany from Estonia, met my now girlfriend in Vienna for an innocuous cup of tea with a side of spaghetti, splashed around on a rooftop pool at Rudas Turkish bath house in Budapest and, more locally, got to see one of the hidden gems of the United States in Charleston with a girl I had met in Atlanta... Go figure. It was a topsy turvy year but I appreciated it and it all had led me to this very moment. I found myself at my desk, peculiar coffee in hand, and ready to copy some soccer game results from Laenderspiel. A deep breath was needed.

Holly fuck. I wasn't quite savvy or aware enough at the time but in retrospect I could have paid someone to gather the 1000's of games I needed or used some sort of web crawler that could extract the results from the web pages but unfortunately none of that crossed my mind. I didn't really know how many games I needed to collect. I just had the mindset of the more the better!

I began the journey of collecting all of the meaningful matches for all of the International conferences. These conferences including:

- UEFA – Union of European Football Associations
- CONMEBOL – Confederacion Sudamericana de Futbol
- CONCACAF – Confederation of North, Central American and Caribbean Association Football
- AFA – Asian Football Confederation
- CAF – Confederation of African Football

- OFC – Oceania Football Confederation

Hour after hour I collected match data and then more match data. And by hour after hour I mean two hours because that is all the mind numbing collecting I could do that first day. I started in Europe because that's where the most teams in any one conference would be coming from. There would be 14 European teams of the 32 competing teams. I recorded the European championships and European World Cup Qualifying games and my goal was to go back to 2004 so I could get 3 full World Cup cycles.

Now what most people don't know is why are certain teams in the World Cup and why are other teams not in the World Cup? Well that's because the World Cup is not just a thing that just drops to us out of the sky every four years. Take the World Cup in Russia for example. That tournament will take place in the middle of June 2018 and go a month but it only consists of 32 teams. What gives? Where's the USA? Where are the Netherlands and Italy? What those 32 teams represent in Russia are 32 very deserving teams that have progressed for the past two years through their respective qualifying groups and conferences and are now able to share their success with the world while participating in the final tournament, where inter-continental play takes place.

2004 would include the European tournament in the summer and then the start to the qualifying cycle for the World Cup in Germany taking place not in 2004, not in 2005, but in 2006. It's a long road to World Cup! I collected the teams, the score, and if someone had home field advantage. Often at tournaments such as the European tournament, that takes place every four years, they're played on neutral sites. Game by game I went collecting data. Sometimes before work, and virtually always after work.

Occasionally I would spot check the data with an official FIFA site to make sure the scores were correct. And while I didn't find many I did find some mistakes believe it or not on Laenderspiel. I don't really blame them. It has to be tough getting all the games right when there are 1000's of games. But this brings me to another important point, and one that I often hear in my actuarial work, which is, "garbage in, garbage out." If you're basing important decisions off of specific data you better feel confident in the source of the data. While I was in general comfortable with the scores I knew in the back of my head I had found some errors.

One's findings and decisions may be perfectly sound given the data but if one is basing the results off of the assumption that the data is accurate and one learns that the data is not then where do you end up? It'd be like loading a city map of Tokyo and using it to navigate you through Charlotte, NC. It can be incredibly dangerous to use faulty data. It can cost money, people's time, and in other more important cases it can cost lives. Remember, "garbage in, garbage out."

This went on for weeks. African Cup of Nations. Who cares who won between Equatorial Guinea and Egypt? I did and in those few weeks of collecting I could have regurgitated many of the African cities that hosted games. Who cares who won between Syria and Australia as Australia switched into qualifying for the World Cup through Asia instead of Oceania? I did. No game was too meaningless. I did this at the office (obviously outside of working hours), at Starbucks after work, and at home until I had over 2000 games results stretching from 2004 to 2017. It was an impressive list and I had collected them all.

The data for international appearances was also on that site. After I started recording these values I quickly realized, this too, would be a huge time suck. It was tedious work changing the time frame and country on Laenderspiel and then recording it in Excel. Unlike collecting the score information myself I, instead, decided to pay my friend Ashley to record them for me. This was arguably the best $80 I've ever spent. I just paid her, came home after work, and the appearances had been recorded.

Who do you think has the most international appearances as a footballing team? I probably would have guessed England or Brazil as that's who I think of first when I think of soccer. And while those would be great guesses those wouldn't be the top dog. Since January of 1900 England has participated in 930 games while Brazil has participated in 998 games, not too shabby. But Sweden, yes Sweden, at 1021 games takes that honor. Maybe massive international experience, engrained in their soccer culture, had a hand in knocking Italy out of the 2018 World Cup. Yes, if you're wondering why you didn't see the Italians in the World Cup for the first time in some 60+ years it's because those pesky, well organized, Swedes knocked them out.

How to Make Sense of It All

I was first going to try to replicate what Szymanski and Kuper did for Soccernomics. I was going to see if I could figure out a regression model using country statistics including GDP/capita, population, and international appearances by country to predict goal differential. They found that those three factors contributed about 25% of the predicted goal differential. While I was on a search to account for more than 25% of the predicted goal differential it was a great place to start. I had some ideas that had been touched upon in their books. The salaries of the players was an interesting variable but the thought of having to go through each game and figure out how much money the team's total salary, average salary, or median salary seemed daunting. Can you imagine having to go through and find the salaries of all the players for Ethiopia or Singapore that played in each of their games? In retrospect I probably didn't look hard enough for that information as there's probably some database somewhere that has all that information. I also had a slightly more qualitative idea at the time wanting to look at percentage of the starters playing in one of the big four leagues, including the English Premier League, the Italian Serie A, the German Bundesliga, and La Liga which is the Spanish league. My thought was the more players you had playing in, what most considered, the best leagues the better your country's team probably was.

Kuper and Szymanski were on a mission to figure out which countries utilize their resources most effectively. So which countries had a consistently better goal differential than what was predicted by the regression model looking at those three factors. As I said earlier they found certain countries used their resources quite well (Brazil, Iceland, Croatia...) while others underperformed (China, India, etc...). The thought behind those factors were as follows: 1) As a country gets wealthier they'll have more surplus to spend and invest in soccer development. Or at least not being in extreme poverty, or a civil war, would be beneficial to your country's soccer success. 2) The more people you have in a country there'd be more soccer players to choose from and thus the team would be better (so China...). 3) The more exposure a country has to foreign competition, and foreign tactics, on the international stage the better as the country can learn from better teams. Fun fact, once again, the country with the most international games is Sweden!

I think, as many have also observed, soccer ideologies are converging as countries get more exposure to other successful countries. Think of all the players going to fine tune their trade now in Europe and how that affects their country of origin. Take the Dutchmen Johan Cruyff, the three-time Ballon D'Or winner, as an example. He is associated with the ideology known as Total Football. The idea of Total Football is one of fast moving, dynamically flowing players moving in sync without real limitations in where any one player should be and positions being more of a formality. If one person leaves his general area to attack a teammate fills in. Unlike many great players Cruyff was also a great coach and manager. After his playing career he took the Dutch Total Football to Barcelona as a coach. He has been widely credited with turning that club around. He was focused on the importance of maintaining possession of the ball throughout the game. If our team has the ball the whole time it's very hard for the opposition to score. This sounds simple enough. Some would argue it was this mentality that morphed into tiki taka football which has been used by Messi's Barcelona for much of the last decade as well as being a large component to the Spanish National Team which found World Cup euphoria in South Africa in 2010 against, who else but, the Dutch. This tika taka football is at times unpleasant to watch as the players pass a ton and move but often don't take chances and go forward which can become unpleasant to a neutral spectator. The Spaniards also won European Championships in 2008 against Germany and 2012 against Italy. There was about a 5-year window where, for what it's worth, I say that Barcelona team was the best club team I've seen and that Spanish team was the best country team I've ever seen.

Part III

Starting the Exploratory Phase

As I started acquiring more and more variables I was really thinking that I needed something more. After all the foundation that I was working with only explained about 25% of the goal differential. Not sure I was willing to bet a meaningful amount of money on 25% predictive power, even though that's not as low as many may think.

The Soccernomics authors were answering a fundamentally different question than myself. They were asking which countries utilized their resources effectively, or ineffectively, and I was just interested in who would win. I didn't care about how many people a country had or how rich they were if it didn't majorly contribute to the actual outcome. I just cared what variables were good predictors for winning. Plain and simple. It was a feel-good feeling knowing that a small country in Iceland, with roughly 330 thousand people, could compete and was great at beating their predicted goal differential in many of their matchups but all that would mean is that they may be just losing by less than would have been predicted. I was interested in winning. The three factors they looked at may very well be included in the end product but I thought I needed something extra. A sweetener, some would say.

Ideally, like I've said before, I would have liked to have gone game by game and calculated the salaries of the starting 11 for each side, and maybe the next iteration of the model I will find a semi painless way to get all this information. Can you imagine scouring the web for the salaries for the starting 11 of Equatorial Guinea for each of their starters for their 2007 games? And then again in 2008? And in 2009? You probably get the point but that's a lot of player information that I would need, and I just didn't have the resources quite yet to do it. In retrospect I could have found some college kids that were interested in this and could have let them help but at the time that didn't really go through my mind.

I had read a study, also in Soccernomics, in the English Premier League that the salaries accounted for an overwhelming majority of the deviation, about 90%, of where teams finished in the premier league. Meaning if you stuck me as the Manchester City coach we'd have a decent shot of winning the league. Teams that spent more on salaries finished towards the top! Shocking! Now I'm not saying this would absolutely produce similar results because there are many things to consider when it comes to compensation from country to country. Business is conducted differently in different countries and there are some external perks of playing in certain countries that cannot be captured by salary alone. For example, some of the Chinese league players are getting paid crazy amounts of money, as they try to build the popularity of the sport in that massively populated country, but if those same players were to go to a different league they may only be able to fetch a fraction of what they're getting paid in China. To illustrate Argentine Carlos Tevez, as of 2017, was the highest paid player in the Chinese Super League at a whopping 37.5 million Euros per year. To round out the top 5 we have the Brazilians Oscar and Hulk, Belgian Axel Witsel, and Italian Pelle making 24.4, 20, 16, and 15 million Euros per year respectively. While Italy failed to make the 2018 World Cup all together, so Pelle didn't even have a chance, only Axel Witsel of those top five earners played for his country in the 2018 World Cup. This just shows that salaries could be distorted going across countries. That being said if one team's starters combined for 44 million per year and another only (I feel bad saying "only" here) 20 million per year one would think that the team that's making 44 million per year would be expected to win.

I looked back on a World Cup draw simulator that I had made a few months prior. Reflecting on this now it really feels quite nerdish. I was basically trying to see if there were certain teams that were more likely to match up with others during the World Cup draw. Before I answer that let me paint the picture for the draw. You have a bunch of rich dudes, mostly Swiss as FIFA is headquartered there, and former players and coaches on a stage in Russia taking turns as they dramatically draw big white balls that have the country names listed on paper inside, basically like opening a fortune cookie, from 4 lottery bins. This is the process that shapes how the World Cup journey will be for each team. And, of course, between drawings there is over analysis done, as this tournament is still about 6 months in the future, and long advertisements, but I digress.

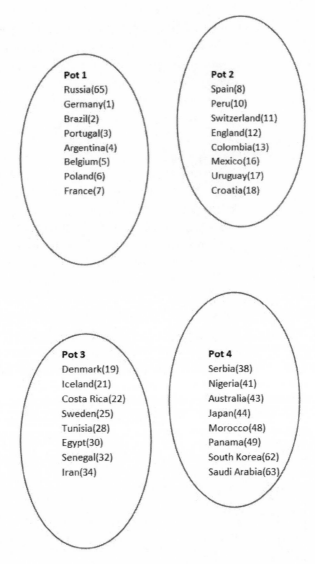

Pot 1
Russia(65)
Germany(1)
Brazil(2)
Portugal(3)
Argentina(4)
Belgium(5)
Poland(6)
France(7)

Pot 2
Spain(8)
Peru(10)
Switzerland(11)
England(12)
Colombia(13)
Mexico(16)
Uruguay(17)
Croatia(18)

Pot 3
Denmark(19)
Iceland(21)
Costa Rica(22)
Sweden(25)
Tunisia(28)
Egypt(30)
Senegal(32)
Iran(34)

Pot 4
Serbia(38)
Nigeria(41)
Australia(43)
Japan(44)
Morocco(48)
Panama(49)
South Korea(62)
Saudi Arabia(63)

Since the 32-team format started in 1998, a World Cup in France and won by France, it had never been conducted like this one in Russia. This go around the 32 teams would be divided into 8 groups of 4, groups A thru H, based on FIFA ranking, and that factor alone, except for the low ranked Russian hosts who would be privileged to be in pot 1 getting the A1 slot.

You will notice in the above graphic the country name and their corresponding FIFA ranking from the draw in parenthesis (although the draw was conducted in early December they use October FIFA rankings to seed). Some of you may be asking where are numbers 9, 14,15, 20, etc...? Those omissions could lead to a few thoughts. It could underline that making it through is often a function of who your qualifying group consists of and maybe a lucky draw on a play in game. It could simply illustrate how tough it is to get to the World Cup and that certain conferences are underrepresented. Should South America only get five teams in? It also could show that these FIFA rankings, while a formulaic measuring stick, could have some faults. Regardless of what it means this World Cup would be without the likes of highly ranked teams such as Chile (9), Wales (14), Italy (15), and the Netherlands (20).

There were stipulations, which were not unique to this tournament, that no more than 2 European teams could be in a single group and no more than 1 team from each of the other conferences could be in a single group. This is after all the World Cup. We wouldn't want a group of just African teams or just European teams, even though it may be more competitive initially, as they play each other all the time. The cool thing about the World Cup is you get teams playing meaningful games against opponents they rarely face.

Are there certain teams that are more likely to draw others? Yes. For instance, because Serbia was the only European team in pot 4 and there were only 2 non-European teams, Brazil and Argentina, in pot 1 Serbia was slightly more likely to be matched up with Brazil or Argentina as the other 6 European teams in pot 1 would have to not pick European teams from pot 2 or 3 to have a chance to be matched with Serbia. Long story short Serbia was more likely to draw 2nd ranked Brazil or 4th ranked Argentina than a truly random draw. In this case a random draw would have been 1/8th as there are 8 teams in each pot. Serbia, sure enough, was drawn with the powerhouse Brazil. While many thought it was a complete waste of time, since I couldn't really bet on teams before the draw was conducted, it turned out to be a good exercise. And the information that I paused on was how the draw was conducted.

In the prior World Cup, as many before it, the first pot consisted of the host country and the other top 7 teams in the world by FIFA ranking. Pots 2 thru 4 were then formed by region trying to explicitly accomplish geographic diversification from the onset, with small exceptions such as the lowest team in Europe getting sent to the African bucket in 2014, oddly enough being France. This format oftentimes led to lopsided groups, albeit geographically diverse, and a group or two that really stood out as very tough. This often, and by often I mean like every time, led to a group being dubbed, "The Group of Death." The USA had the task of being in the group of death in 2014 with the historical American kryptonite in Ghana, Cristiano Ronaldo's Portugal, and eventual champions Germany.

What is FIFA's job after all? They strive for their product to be competitive and try to put on entertaining matchups. Their job is to produce compelling matchups and one would think they want, and I would agree with, great teams playing at the very end. Would they want 3 teams in the top 15 to be playing each other in the group stage? While it would make for compelling matchups early on, and while satisfying geographic diversification, it would not allow all three great teams to get out of the group stage. That would have certainly been a Group of Death. They must have faith that the FIFA rankings, albeit being slightly biased towards their own rankings, would be a good indicator of how the games will go. In the new format you'd never see three top 15 ranked teams in the same group. This would, on a cursory level, appear to be fairer and smooth the playing field from group to group. I could get behind this. It would improve the balance of the groups.

What did the draw make me think? FIFA rankings. FIFA rankings capture how a team has been performing and is kind of like a moving average of a stock. Laenderspiel had FIFA rankings by month going back years. And it makes simple intuitive sense. A team ranked 2nd in the world almost certainly will beat a team ranked 114th in the world. It seemed to be a type of variable I was looking for. And it, in my eyes would capture, in some respects, the three variables Soccernomics analyzed as well as things like salaries. One would think the higher salaries the players receive for their club teams would translate to wins for their national team and thus make for better FIFA rankings. The higher differential between FIFA rankings of two sides would likely result in a higher expected goal differential between those two teams. Higher expected goal differential would unsurprisingly increase their probability to win. It's very analogous to viewing the NCAA basketball tournaments with the seedings. It seems obvious in retrospect to use a seeding system but it did not hit me until I took a step back and worked on and saw the World Cup draw.

How are the FIFA rankings currently determined? Simply put it's a point system. Teams acquire points from results. FIFA ranks the points of countries from greatest to least and then you get the FIFA rankings. Points can be calculated from the equation, P=M*I*T*C, where:

P	Points for a given match
M	Match Result
I	Importance
T	Strength of Opposing Team
C	Strength of Confederation

And those variables are defined as follows:

M =	Match Result
3	victory
1	draw
0	loss
2	pk win
1	pk loss

*pk = penalty kick

I =	Importance
1	friendly match
2.5	FIFA World Cup™ qualifier or confederation-level qualifier
3	Confederation-level final competition or FIFA Confederations Cup
4	FIFA World Cup™ final competition

T = Strength of Opposing Team
200 - (opposition ranking)
Caveats
Playing the top team is a 200, min value of 50 (for opposing teams ranked 150 or worse)

C = The strength of a confederation is calculated on the basis of the number of victories by that confederation at the last three FIFA World Cup™ competitions.	Strength of Confederation
Currently	
CONMEBOL	1
UEFA	0.99
AFC/CAF/OFC/CONCACAF	0.85

The points from the last four years are then weighted to produce what is commonly referred to as a weighted moving average. Those weights follow the table below:

Average points go back 4 years	
current year	100%
previous year	50%
for year 3	30%
for year 4	20%
older than 4 years	0%

As a quick example let's say a country has:
200 points this year
150 points in the prior year
100 for the year three years ago
250 for the year four years ago

$1*200 + .5*150 + .3*100 + .2*250 = 355$ points

Let's swap the prior year's points with the points from four years ago in the prior example to see how the resulting points change. Below, one can see that more recent success is rewarded in this framework. Success four years ago, while taken into consideration, is not as heavily rewarded as more recent success.

$1*200 + .5*\mathbf{250} + .3*100 + .2*\mathbf{150} = 385$ points

This FIFA ranking method that I considered undertaking was not without issues though. Prior to 06 the FIFA rankings were based off an average of the last 8 years of games with different weightings for the current scheme, different types of matches, the opponent's ranking, which conference the opponent came from, and how far back in time the game was played. For example, a win against Vanuatu in a friendly match was not worth the same points as beating Spain in the World Cup. After the Germany 06 World Cup this was slightly altered by only looking at the last 4 years of games, thus only including one World Cup cycle instead of two World Cup cycles. This was one problem as my FIFA rankings weren't going to be apples to apples when looking at prior 06 data to post 06 data. A FIFA ranking of 17 in 2003 was fundamentally different than looking at a FIFA ranking of 17 in 2018.

Challenge two was that in the FIFA ranking system teams get points for friendlies, albeit a quarter of the points that would be received compared to a World Cup game but points nonetheless. As there are points on the line and the points determine the seeding for qualifying campaigns teams are incentivized to meticulously schedule somewhat easier opponents in hopes of getting better seeding. Some countries really try to challenge themselves against better opposition during friendlies but certain teams really try to navigate the system to their advantage. I decided to not include friendlies because I, like many others, view friendlies as more of experimental settings where a manager can give chances to players that do not typically see game time.

Like I mentioned before beating opponents in different conferences also has different weightings. Beating a European or South American team is better for getting points than beating a team in Asia all else being equal. And since meaningful intercontinental play between World Cups is rare it doesn't give much chance for teams in the "weaker" conferences to advance. Since UEFA and CONMEBOL have greater weights we often see clumps of European and South American teams in the top 10-20. They have better weightings because those conferences have tended to perform better in World Cups. If the 2018 semi-final happened to be composed of Mexico, Iran, Egypt, and Senegal it'd be a safe bet that those conference weightings would change.

Another issue is that Russia, as they don't have to qualify, doesn't get a chance to move up or down in the 4 years leading up to the World Cup. Russia's only major tournament since the last World Cup in 2014 was the European Championships in 2016. In that tournament they tied just one game to England and lost the other two to Slovakia and Wales. The real meaningful games in the last four years they did not perform well. As friendlies aren't given as much baring as World Cup qualifiers we don't really have a comprehensive picture of what Russia is or would be. Russia was ranked as the weakest team in their own World Cup. It's hard to say where they would have ended up if they had to qualify. Most were saying simply, "they wouldn't have qualified."

While it's been discussed, and appears quite likely, to change the FIFA ranking system and while I do agree with a lot of the changes I, quite selfishly, don't want them to as this means me having to acquire even more data going forward as I would have to come up with a method to convert these "old" FIFA rankings into the corresponding new method ranking. I'll save that challenge for when it's confirmed. The next iteration will most likely involve some new ranking and hopefully it doesn't penalize teams for taking friendlies against better opponents.

Let's Get Some Predicted Goal Differential up in Here!

This would be the pivotal phase to set the stage for the rest of the model. The predicted goal differential would drive how we estimate the probabilities and thus how we figure out which bets seem to be bargains. I looked at a lot of different variables and different combinations. FIFA rankings squared, cubed, square rooted, and the list goes on...

Home field advantage ended up being a very interesting undertaking. It seemed simple at first. I wanted to answer how many goals does a team get to start with for just being home. Most would agree that most countries have an advantage by playing at home in front of their fans but how much was this advantage worth? Was it .2, .5, or some other goals per game?

I was seeing that home field advantage is quite different from continent to continent. It seemed to be much greater outside of Europe. It appeared that being home in a European vs European game was good for about .3 goals per game where as being home in a South American vs another South American team, or another intra continental matchup, was good for about .6 goals per game.

Are European teams better overall? Do they just have less weaker teams leading to fewer blowout matchups? Are there just less goals scored there? Well let's look. Below you'll see a table of the average number of combined goals scored in those conference matchups, once again excluding friendlies. On average about 2.60 goals are scored in a South American matchup which is actually less than in Europe, at 2.74. What we're saying is there are less goals scored in South American matchups even though we're seeing that home field advantage is worth much more in a South American matchup than in Europe. It's not just that there are fewer goals, in general, scored in European matchups. So how could or why would this be?

Games with a Home Field Advantage Since 2004	
Conference	Average Total Goals Scored
CAF	2.55
CONMEBOL	2.60
AFC	2.67
UEFA	2.74
CONCACAF	3.08

Now I can't say for certain but I have a couple educated guesses. In Europe the infrastructure is better and the distances between countries tend to be closer. The proximity and good traveling routes encourage fans from the away team to travel to see their team play in other countries. On the other hand, you have places like Brazil. Brazil is a big country and for traveling fans to get there requires a flight or a very long drive. Although Uruguay borders Brazil the distance from Montevideo to Rio is still about 2,400 km. That's crazy! You know how many countries are within a 2,400 km radius of Vienna in

Austria, albeit the "Heart of Europe"? Of the 36 teams that participated in European qualification every country is within 2,400 km of Vienna except for Iceland, Israel, Kazakhstan, and Georgia. Georgia was the only one of those four that were part of Austria's qualifying group meaning Austria never had to worry about traveling to the other three. Point in being that European fans, in general, don't have to travel as far to see their team play opposing teams.

In South America you have some countries that are very unique in terms of where they play or should I say how high they play. Some countries in South America play at such a high altitude that games in capitals of Bolivia, Ecuador, and Colombia were actually prevented from hosting games in their capitals from May 2007 to May 2008 because they were greater than 2,500 meters (8,200 ft) above sea level. FIFA saw it as a huge home field advantage and some were concerned about the players' health, as many players can be seen strapped to oxygen tanks after games.

After looking at combinations of variables and different data splits, including the different conferences and splitting before and after the FIFA ranking observation window change in 2006 from 8 years to 4 years, I would make a couple model variations that typically included some or all the variables below:

- Home Field Advantage
    o Did a team have a home field advantage? Yes = 1 or No = 0
- Start of year FIFA ranking
    o The team's starting January FIFA ranking going into the year
- Momentum factor
    o Team's January FIFA ranking minus the prior June's FIFA ranking

- Thought was that even if a team had slipped a bit in recent history maybe they were prone to an uptick or vice versa

One may ask how predictive these variables were on goal differential, which in my study was the dependent variable. Once again it varied from conference to conference. The linear regression on the goal differential had a higher R squared value within European matchups, almost 70%. R squared can be thought of as how close our actual data is to what would be predicted by our best fit line. R squared is a value from 0% to 100%. If you had a 100% R squared value that would mean whatever variables you were working with would lead to matching exactly the dependent variable you were trying to find, in our case goal differential. R squared can be thought of as "(explained variation)/(total variation)". Remember the Soccernomics' study was about 25%. Said another way they had found variables that explained a quarter of the goal differential. Unfortunately, the other conferences did not match as closely as Europe at 70%. The others were between 50% and 60%.

Going forward I will stick with illustrating one such model that I referred to as the "UEFA Add Momentum" model and I think its properties can best be reveled through a couple of examples.

UEFA Add Momentum Coefficients

	FIFA Rankings (January) 1	FIFA Rankings (January) 2
Europe	-0.021	0.021
Non Europe	-0.0195	0.0195
Default	-0.0206	0.0206

	FIFA Ranking Momentum Change (Prior June to Jan) 1	FIFA Ranking Momentum Change (Prior June to Jan) 2
Europe	0.008	-0.008
Non Europe	0.0117	-0.0117
Default	0.0100	-0.0100

	Home (1)/Neutral Site (0)
Europe	0.3
Non Europe	0.58
Default	0.4

In the coefficients table above you'll see how our variables go into predicting goal differential. There are three splits. One is for a European vs European matchup, the row marked as "Europe". One is for an intra-conference battle outside of Europe, the row marked as "Non Europe". The last is for an inter-conference battle, the row marked as "Default". Let's look at how these get applied in a couple matchups.

Possible World Cup Matchup Between European Sides – Russia vs Spain

Team 1 (Home Team if applicable)	Team 2 (Away Team if applicable)	Team 1 Conference	Team 2 Conference	Location	FIFA Rankings (January) 1	FIFA Rankings (January) 2	FIFA Ranking Momentum Change (Prior June to Jan) 1	FIFA Ranking Momentum Change (Prior June to Jan) 2	Home (1)/Neutral Site (0)
Russia	Spain	UEFA	UEFA	Russia	62	6	-1	-4	1

It's just plugging and chugging at this point (Excel can do this for you with some if statements combined with some sumproduct functions). To clarify Spain's Momentum Change of -4 just means that back in June of the prior year they were ranked 10, or 6 - -4. Since these are both European teams we'll use the coefficients in the first row of the coefficients table:

$$(-.021 * 62) + (.021 * 6) + (.008 * -1) + (-.008 * -4) + (.3 * 1) = -.852$$

With this model Russia is expected to lose to Spain by .852 goals. Note in this case that the home field variable is equal to 1 since Russia is playing in Russia. Let's now look at what it would predict for an inter-conference battle.

Possible World Cup Inter-Conference Battle – Argentina vs Switzerland

Team 1 (Home Team if applicable)	Team 2 (Away Team if applicable)	Team 1 Conference	Team 2 Conference	Location	FIFA Rankings (January) 1	FIFA Rankings (January) 2	FIFA Ranking Momentum Change (Prior June to Jan) 1	FIFA Ranking Momentum Change (Prior June to Jan) 2	Home (1)/Neutral Site (0)
Argentina	Switzerland	CONMEBOL	UEFA	Russia	4	8	2	-1	0

Since this is an inter-conference battle we'll use the coefficients in the third row of the coefficients table:

$$(-.0206 * 4) + (.0206 * 8) + (.01 * 2) + (-.01 * -1) + (.4 * 0) = .1124$$

In this case Argentina is favored by .1124 goals. Note in this case the home field variable is equal to 0 since this matchup is happening in Russia. While having these predicted goal differentials is all cool and dandy we'll need to convert the goal differentials into probabilities of winning, tying, and losing to help us with our bets.

All Bout da Buckets

While I looked at different variations of the coefficients this general method was the same for all the model variations. Now I must give my actuarial training props when they're due and this was definitely a time my studying of death modeling came in handy. One strategy actuaries use when modeling reserves and when claims will be paid, to cut down on runtime and data, is to let one age in a band of ages represent that whole band. Often the age bands are in groups of 5 years but could be more or less depending on the precision wanted. For instance, instead of modeling the policies below they may just assume 14,700 policies are age 34 as they make up the highest percentage of the band. Still others would make all the policies the middle year of the band, or 33 in this group. Getting more policies in a group also improves credibility concerns.

Age	# of Policies	% of Band
31	4000	27%
32	2500	17%
33	1000	7%
34	5700	39%
35	1500	10%
Total	14700	

What I did with mapping goal differential to probabilities had the above method in mind. I wanted to create buckets that addressed some of the credibility questions I had and simplified the data. What I did was I put all the games where the teams were predicted to be within 0 and .1 goals together, between .1 and .2 goals together, between .2 and .3 goals, and so on and so forth into buckets and mapped them to the midpoints of the ranges (ex: the 0 to .1 goal bucket was mapped to .05). I used these bucketed probabilities as the basis of the whole model.

Below is the UEFA Add Momentum model. The darkest dots (going up and to the right) show the win percentage with respect to the predicted goal differential, on the horizontal axis. The lightest dots show the loss percentage with respect to the predicted goal differential. And lastly, the medium-dark dots show the tie percentage with respect to the predicted goal differential (go to betisround.com to see more of these types of charts in color). Not too surprisingly the win percentage, looking at the darkest dots, increases with expected goal differential while tying and losing drops. When a team is predicted to win by about three goals they appear to have about guaranteed victory.

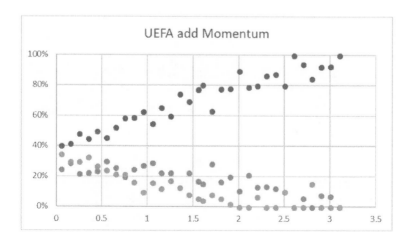

Now there are a couple things to notice and keep in mind. These details, you may think, should have been dealt with differently and in the next iteration of models I may alter some or all of them.

In the above scatterplot you'll see that the percentage of tying is teetering between 20-30% for most predicted goal differentials between 0 and 1.5 and then starts to tail off as the predicted goal differential increases over 1.5. I will admit to questioning how I handled games decided by penalty kicks in the recorded games. If there was a penalty kick shootout during a game some would say that I should have marked that down as a tie because if one were betting in Vegas it would considered a tie if it goes into a shootout. I, however, gave a win to whoever actually won the game by giving an extra goal to the winning side. While very few games that I recorded went into pk's, as this was basically just prior World Cups and conference tournaments since qualifiers can end in ties, there were some. Long story short, in my mind I thought I may be slightly underestimating the percentage of ties that could happen.

Throughout my whole data set I had about 22% of games ending in ties while not counting the penalty kicks as a draw. For historical reference the 2010 South Africa World Cup group stage had 14 of the 48 games end in draws, or about 29%. The 2014 Brazil World Cup group stage had 9 of the 48 games end in draws, or about 19%. And as I'm writing this after the Russian World Cup, like in Brazil, 9 of the 48 games ended in draws, once again at about 19%.

Now I needed a way to explicitly convert the predicted goal differential into a probability of winning, probability of losing, and a probability of tying. This would be called a trendline or a best fit line. One thing I had to force in was the intercepts. If two teams are dead even the chances of them winning vs losing should be the same. I wanted trendlines that matched the data well and wanted to keep in mind that the matchups during the World Cup were going to be concentrated in the 0 to 1 goal differential range. There wasn't going to be many huge spread games. The Vanuatu's and Malta's of the World had already been sent home.

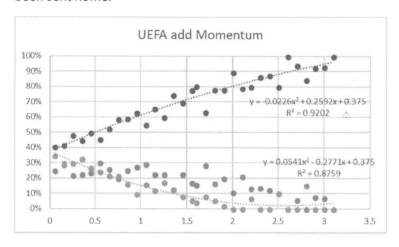

Since I had to force the trendlines for winning and losing's intercepts, the tie percentage would be backed out. Using da lingo, the probability of a tie would be "the plug". I could now calculate how often, for example, a team that was predicted to win by .28 goals should win vs tie vs lose. In the above chart our y, or dependent variable, was the corresponding probability and our x was the predicted goal differential. When Uruguay was projected to beat Egypt by .1248 goals Uruguay's probability of winning, and thus Egypt's probability of losing, was:

-0.0226 * (.1248)^2 + 0.2592 * (.1248) + 0.375 = .406996 or about 41%

Uruguay's probability of losing, and thus Egypt's probability of winning, was:

$0.0541 * (.1248)^2 - 0.2771 * (.1248) + 0.375 = .341261$ or about 34%

The compliment of those two probabilities, or about 25% (100% - 41% - 34%), was the probability that Uruguay and Egypt would tie. When this game played out on June 15th, I of course was delaying going to work as I sat at Not Another Broken Egg café's counter, hands getting tighter and tighter, hoping Egypt could get away with at least a point. It looked like a draw was going to be the result until an 89th minute goal by defender Jose Gimenez. Heartbreaking. It was heartbreaking for the Egypt faithful, the Egyptian team, and unfortunately for our Egypt to advance from the group stage bet. So close, so close. But that is after all soccer. It's sometimes so beautiful but other times so cruel. I was slightly happy we didn't bet what we were originally going to on Egypt as, one of our worries came to fruition, Mo Salah didn't play. As they say, "the ball is round…"

The Matrix (The Movie Wishes It Could Be This Cool)

I wrote a macro in VBA to help me with this task. Macros are basically little, or sometimes very big, routines that one can write within Microsoft Excel to automate mundane and tedious tasks. It can save crazy amounts of time. If you wanted to fill in a multiplication table you could write a little program, I'm talking in pseudocode, that goes across the rows and says take the first number in this row and multiply it by whatever number is above where I'm at in this column. I've written macros to simulate different risks occurring in tandem at an insurance company as well as finding combinations of American football players to choose on a budget for daily fantasy leagues like DraftKings and FanDuel. Macros, and programming in general, are so helpful! Instead of manually having to go through one by one all 32 teams playing the other 31 teams I wrote a simple looping program to do all of that for me. The macro would bring in, for example, Poland and Senegal and look up their accompanying information which would feed into predicting the goal differential which would then be turned into probabilities that would be recorded in my matrix.

Keep in mind the only teams that are guaranteed to face off against each other are the teams in a country's group. As a refresher, the World Cup consists of 8 groups of 4. Every country is guaranteed to play the group stage games against each team in their group. Thus, each team is guaranteed to play at least 3 games. This 32 by 32 matrix had probabilities for every possible matchup. While Panama vs Saudi Arabia in the knockout stages was incredibly unlikely it was still populated in the matrix. Here's Group H, a small piece of that big 32 by 32 matrix:

	Poland	Japan	Senegal	Colombia
Poland		58%	46%	38%
Japan	18%		25%	18%
Senegal	29%	50%		29%
Colombia	37%	58%	46%	

This table isn't exactly intuitive, so I will explain. Take for example Poland in row 1. As one goes across that first row those percentages are revealing the percentage of times I'm predicting Poland would beat those other teams. Conversely if one starts in the Poland column and goes down that is illustrating how often those corresponding row teams would beat Poland. My model is giving Poland a 46% chance to win against Senegal. And how much is it giving for Senegal to beat Poland? Yes, 29%. So how about a tie between Poland and Senegal? That is the complement to what we already know, 100% - 46% - 29%, or 25%. How about a tie between Colombia and Japan? That would be 100%-58%-18% or 24%. One interesting insight that came from doing this analysis is that the percentage for a tie between most matchups didn't deviate too much; it was almost always 24 or 25%.

Simulate the World Cup... and Again... and Again... and Again... and Well You Get the Picture

Below we have group E, consisting of the tournament favorites Brazil. This was also a group of mass importance, as I would later find out, as two of our biggest bets came from this group.

	Brazil	Serbia	Costa Rica	Switzerland
Brazil		58%	49%	41%
Serbia	18%		27%	21%
Costa Rica	26%	48%		30%
Switzerland	34%	55%	45%	

Now let's simulate the tournament for group E. Presented below in figure Da Simulation Group E Matchday 1 you'll see what look to be a bunch of gibberish numbers. To some extent you'd be correct. If by gibberish you mean random then you'd be correct. The numbers in the copper orange are random numbers from excel's handy dandy random number generator function, which can be attained by using the function rand() in Excel (one could spend a long time looking into just how random certain "random number generators" are). There is a point to all these numbers, and if you glance up at the previous matrix you may be able to pick them out yourself. You'll see .411755 in the column to the right of Brazil and in the matrix above you will see it gives Brazil a 42% chance to beat Switzerland. Similarly, the .336324 next to Switzerland corresponds to the 34% in the matrix illustrating that Switzerland has a 34% chance of beating Brazil. Below .411755 and .336324 is .251921 which is the implied probability of Brazil and Switzerland tying. Moving another column over to the right we have the cumulative distribution of what our possible outcomes are. The .748079 can be translated into the fact that, according to the model, there's about a 75% chance that either Brazil or Switzerland win outright.

We're going to utilize the random decimal, from 0 to 1, to simulate the game. If our random number is between 0 and .411755 we'll assign that as a win for Brazil resulting in 3 points for Brazil and 0 points for Switzerland. A number between .411755 and .748079 we'll assign that as a win for Switzerland. And last, but not least, a number between .748079 and 1 will be a tie giving both teams 1 point. You can see in this simulation for the first set of games in group E my model would have had Brazil and Switzerland tying while Costa Rica would have beaten Serbia. Keep in mind every random number is independent from all the other random numbers that are being generated. Each time one clicks calculate in Excel a new random number is generated and the next time it may be a .2 in the Brazil Switzerland Matchup which would, instead, result in a Brazil win.

Figure Da Simulation Group E Matchday 1

E	Matchday 1			0	0.874743
Team 1	Brazil	0.411755	0.411755		
Team 2	Switzerland	0.336324	0.748079		
		0.251921	1		
					3
			Team 1		1
			Team 2		1
				0	0.150008
Team 3	Costa Rica	0.478916	0.478916		
Team 4	Serbia	0.269089	0.748005		
		0.251995	1		
					1
			Team 3		3
			Team 4		0

Figure Da Simulation Group E Matchday 2

E	Matchday 2			0	0.211478
Team 1	Brazil	0.485869	0.485869		
Team 3	Costa Rica	0.262404	0.748272		
		0.251728	1		
					1
			Team 1	3	
			Team 3	0	
				0	0.486064
Team 2	Switzerland	0.546503	0.546503		
Team 4	Serbia	0.206534	0.753037		
		0.246963	1		
					1
			Team 2	3	
			Team 4	0	

Above, our matchday 2 simulations would have resulted in Brazil getting the 3 points against Costa Rica and Switzerland getting the 3 points against Serbia.

Figure Da Simulation Group E Matchday 3

E	Matchday 3			0	0.670847
Team 1	Brazil	0.581417	0.581417		
Team 4	Serbia	0.176522	0.75794		
		0.24206	1		
					2
			Team 1		0
			Team 4		3
				0	0.011319
Team 2	Switzerland	0.45107	0.45107		
Team 3	Costa Rica	0.296397	0.747466		
		0.252534	1		
					1
			Team 2		3
			Team 3		0

Lastly, our matchday 3 simulations would have resulted in Serbia upsetting Brazil, given just an 18% chance of winning, and Switzerland handling business against Costa Rica.

So that round of simulations would have resulted in the table below (the Brazilian fans would be furious, or possibly pleasantly optimistic depending on their potential path to the final). One valid criticism of this method is that I don't explicitly or implicitly calculate the scores in each matchup. This leads to an issue in how I handle ties in the group standings. Maybe for the next World Cup I'll try to model this or maybe you can find a way to model it! For this version I used another random number generator for each team and ordered them that way, which crazily enough I would later find out is essentially how Japan advanced over Senegal. For the first time in the World Cup's present format a team advanced to the knockout stage, Japan, because they had less yellow cards than another team,

Senegal. I don't want to sound bitter but group H also cost us a fair bit of money, but once again I digress.

In the following Switzerland and Brazil would advance to the round of 16 and they'd play the runners up and winners of group F respectively (group F consists of Germany, South Korea, Sweden, and Mexico).

E		Points
Team 2	Switzerland	7
Team 1	Brazil	4
Team 3	Costa Rica	3
Team 4	Serbia	3

Just to illustrate though if Serbia would have tied Costa Rica then it would have been a tossup between Brazil and Serbia advancing as they would have both been on 4 points. This does not seem like a completely realistic assumption and was a known limitation of the model.

While that seems simple enough let's do it for every group. Each group, as you saw above, has 6 games. There is a total of 6 games x 8 groups or 48 group games to simulate. Then I'd need to simulate the round of 16, round of 8, semifinals, and finals for a total of 63 games for the whole tournament (there are technically 64 total games played at the World Cup but I was not concerned with the 3rd place game). So, think of all of the random numbers factoring into how the tournament shakes out and that was just one simulation. I wanted to simulate the whole tournament 5000 times to get a good view on each team's position. And that's exactly what I did. Each iteration of the model I simulated the World Cup 5000 times and recorded what happened in each round. Below is the framework in which we are working in, as seen in Figure Da Tourney. In the above example Switzerland would have landed in the E1 spot and Brazil would have been put in the E2 spot.

Figure Da Tourney

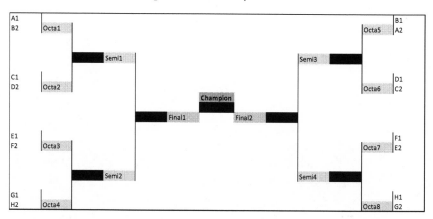

Aw Yeah, Looking at Results

While the raw data is nothing great to look at it contains vast insights and trends by group and throughout the tournament. It's hard to visualize these matchups by yourself because there are so many moving pieces. This method is a concrete way to say if you believe in these probabilities here are the ways the tournament could shake out with actual probabilities and numbers to base your bets off of!

Figure Round of 16 (WA or A1 above = Winner of Group A, RUD or D2 above = Runner Up of Group D)

	WA	RUA	WB	RUB	WC	RUC	WD	RUD	WE	RUE	WF	RUF	WG	RUG	WH	RUH
								Round of 16								
1	Saudi Arabia	Russia	Spain	Iran	France	Peru	Argentina	Nigeria	Brazil	Switzerland	Germany	Sweden	Tunisia	Belgium	Japan	Poland
2	Egypt	Uruguay	Morocco	Portugal	France	Australia	Croatia	Iceland	Costa Rica	Switzerland	Germany	South Korea	England	Panama	Colombia	Poland
3	Russia	Uruguay	Spain	Portugal	Australia	France	Argentina	Iceland	Brazil	Costa Rica	Germany	South Korea	England	Tunisia	Colombia	Poland
4	Egypt	Saudi Arabia	Morocco	Spain	France	Peru	Argentina	Croatia	Costa Rica	Brazil	Germany	South Korea	England	Tunisia	Japan	Colombia
5	Russia	Egypt	Portugal	Iran	Australia	Peru	Argentina	Croatia	Serbia	Costa Rica	Mexico	South Korea	Belgium	England	Poland	Senegal
6	Uruguay	Russia	Portugal	Spain	France	Peru	Argentina	Iceland	Switzerland	Brazil	Mexico	Sweden	Belgium	England	Poland	Colombia
...																
19	Uruguay	Saudi Arabia	Portugal	Iran	France	Peru	Iceland	Argentina	Switzerland	Costa Rica	Mexico	Germany	Belgium	Panama	Senegal	Colombia
20	Saudi Arabia	Russia	Iran	Portugal	Denmark	France	Argentina	Croatia	Costa Rica	Switzerland	Germany	South Korea	England	Panama	Poland	Senegal
45	Egypt	Saudi Arabia	Portugal	Iran	Denmark	France	Iceland	Argentina	Brazil	Switzerland	Sweden	South Korea	England	Tunisia	Japan	Senegal
46	Saudi Arabia	Uruguay	Portugal	Spain	France	Peru	Croatia	Argentina	Switzerland	Brazil	Mexico	Sweden	England	Tunisia	Poland	Japan
...																
2206	Uruguay	Egypt	Portugal	Spain	Peru	Denmark	Iceland	Croatia	Serbia	Costa Rica	Sweden	Germany	England	Tunisia	Colombia	Poland
2207	Egypt	Uruguay	Portugal	Morocco	Peru	Australia	Croatia	Argentina	Costa Rica	Brazil	Germany	Sweden	Belgium	Tunisia	Senegal	Japan
2214	Egypt	Uruguay	Spain	Portugal	Australia	Peru	Argentina	Croatia	Brazil	Costa Rica	Germany	Mexico	England	Croatia	Poland	Senegal
2215	Egypt	Uruguay	Morocco	Spain	Denmark	Australia	Argentina	Croatia	Switzerland	Brazil	Mexico	South Korea	Belgium	Panama	Colombia	Senegal
...																
4993	Egypt	Russia	Portugal	Spain	Peru	Australia	Argentina	Iceland	Brazil	Costa Rica	Mexico	Germany	England	Belgium	Poland	Colombia
4994	Uruguay	Saudi Arabia	Portugal	Spain	France	Peru	Nigeria	Croatia	Switzerland	Brazil	Germany	Mexico	Tunisia	England	Colombia	Poland
4995	Uruguay	Saudi Arabia	Portugal	Iran	Peru	France	Iceland	Argentina	Brazil	Switzerland	Mexico	South Korea	Tunisia	Belgium	Senegal	Poland
4996	Egypt	Russia	Spain	Portugal	Australia	Denmark	Argentina	Iceland	Brazil	Switzerland	Germany	Mexico	Belgium	England	Colombia	Poland
4997	Saudi Arabia	Egypt	Portugal	Spain	Denmark	Peru	Iceland	Argentina	Brazil	Switzerland	Germany	South Korea	Belgium	England	Poland	Japan
4998	Uruguay	Egypt	Portugal	Spain	France	Australia	Croatia	Argentina	Serbia	Switzerland	Germany	Sweden	England	Panama	Colombia	Poland
4999	Saudi Arabia	Egypt	Spain	Portugal	France	Denmark	Argentina	Nigeria	Switzerland	Brazil	Germany	South Korea	Belgium	Tunisia	Poland	Colombia
5000	Uruguay	Egypt	Iran	Spain	Peru	France	Iceland	Nigeria	Brazil	Switzerland	Germany	Sweden	England	Tunisia	Japan	Senegal

Figure Round of 8 (Octa1 is the winner of A1 and B2, see in Da Tourney Figure)

	Octa1	Octa2	Octa3	Octa4	Octa5	Octa6	Octa7	Octa8
				Round of 8				
1	Egypt	Argentina	Costa Rica	Tunisia	Portugal	Croatia	Switzerland	Belgium
2	Saudi Arabia	France	Sweden	Poland	Spain	Peru	Switzerland	Belgium
3	Portugal	Iceland	South Korea	Poland	Morocco	Australia	Germany	Panama
4	Portugal	Iceland	Brazil	Belgium	Uruguay	Argentina	Costa Rica	Colombia
5	Spain	France	South Korea	Colombia	Saudi Arabia	Peru	Germany	Japan
6	Russia	Croatia	Serbia	Belgium	Egypt	Argentina	Mexico	Poland
7	Spain	France	Switzerland	Belgium	Portugal	Peru	Mexico	Poland
8	Portugal	France	Switzerland	Belgium	Egypt	Argentina	Germany	England
9	Morocco	Iceland	South Korea	Belgium	Saudi Arabia	Argentina	Mexico	Tunisia
10	Egypt	Iceland	Brazil	Japan	Spain	Argentina	Switzerland	Poland
...								
4991	Egypt	Argentina	Brazil	England	Spain	Peru	Switzerland	Tunisia
4992	Portugal	Croatia	Switzerland	Senegal	Iran	Nigeria	Costa Rica	Poland
4993	Iran	Denmark	Brazil	Colombia	Uruguay	France	Germany	Poland
4994	Spain	Iceland	Germany	England	Russia	Australia	Mexico	Belgium
4995	Uruguay	Croatia	Mexico	Poland	Portugal	Peru	Germany	England
4996	Uruguay	Argentina	Brazil	Poland	Saudi Arabia	France	Switzerland	Belgium
4997	Egypt	Iceland	Mexico	Belgium	Spain	Denmark	Germany	Colombia
4998	Spain	Argentina	Brazil	Belgium	Portugal	Peru	Switzerland	England
4999	Uruguay	France	Serbia	England	Egypt	Croatia	Germany	Colombia
5000	Portugal	France	Switzerland	Belgium	Egypt	Argentina	Brazil	Poland

Figure Semis

	Semi			
	Semi1	Semi2	Semi3	Semi4
1	Egypt	Costa Rica	Portugal	Switzerland
2	France	Poland	Spain	Switzerland
3	Portugal	Poland	Australia	Germany
4	Portugal	Belgium	Argentina	Colombia
5	Spain	Colombia	Peru	Germany
...				
51	Uruguay	Tunisia	Argentina	Colombia
52	Argentina	Belgium	Portugal	Switzerland
53	Denmark	South Korea	Morocco	Belgium
54	Iran	Sweden	Croatia	Poland
55	Russia	Poland	Iceland	Switzerland
...				
4891	Iceland	Poland	France	Switzerland
4892	Peru	England	Egypt	Poland
4893	Croatia	Switzerland	Spain	Germany
4894	Denmark	Mexico	Portugal	Belgium
4895	Denmark	Senegal	France	Poland
...				
4921	Peru	Japan	France	Serbia
4922	France	Germany	Croatia	Brazil
4923	Spain	Belgium	France	Tunisia
4924	Croatia	Sweden	Iran	Japan
4925	Portugal	Switzerland	France	Germany

With this data I could answer important questions like who has the best chance to get out of their group as well who is most likely to fail to get out of their group. We also wanted to answer who's the most likely to get to the quarterfinals, semifinals, finals, and last of all who is the most likely to be the world champions. At the end of the day I'm searching for value in my picks. I just wanted to be appropriately compensated for the risk I was taking on, and hopefully in the process also find picks that were likely to pay out with a respectable likelihood. Even if the odds seemed well compensated for Saudi Arabia to win it all was it really worth betting something that I think has next to nil probability of happening? It's debatable and depends how risk averse or seeking you are. One has to remember that we're not getting to bet the tournament over a course of 5000 times. We are betting on one tournament. We have one shot.

With this information I was able to compare what my probabilities were vs what was being offered in Vegas (I always use the term Vegas but I really just mean the prevailing odds in the gambling world) in order to understand where the value to be had was. Everything in theory works... We had some things to keep in mind that were working against us:

- Were there injuries that positively or negatively affect odds? For instance, Mo Salah was so pivotal for Egypt lowering their FIFA ranking and making the World Cup. If our projections are based off of FIFA rankings and Mo Salah was a huge contributor to that is it wise to bet the house on an Egypt bet? I would say probably not.
- It's a problem when one is predicting games between teams from different qualifying conferences as they haven't played those teams in a meaningful match for at least 4 years. Since there were 14 European teams and only 8 groups multiple European teams in a group was going to happen but was capped at two European teams per group. Because of more conference data it may be wise to bet slightly more on the groups with two European teams as we could be marginally more confident in how those groups would

unfold. Remember our R squared value was higher in European Matchups.

- The World Cup is a small sample size. Doesn't matter how good our picks are; crazy, unpredictable, things can happen over the short run. Maybe we should put a limit on how much we'd be willing to lose on any single bet? Although 3 games are still not a great sample size it's still bigger than 1, and we may be better off making bets on teams getting out of the group and bets for not getting out of the group instead of single game bets. Even if Brazil were to lose a single game the chances they'd lose multiple and not make it out of the group were small.

Setting the Stage for Placing the Bets

Unsurprisingly many of the big names we thought were over-priced. The bookies are anticipating that people will flock towards the favorites. People that know nothing about soccer will still sometimes say, "Brazil is good, I'll bet them!"

The bets in a group are, on differing degrees, correlated. Take our group B results under this model setup, in order of most likely to least likely:

Winner B	Runner Up B	# out of 5000	Percent
Portugal	Spain	973	19%
Spain	Portugal	932	19%
Portugal	Iran	568	11%
Spain	Iran	518	10%
Portugal	Morocco	373	7%
Iran	Spain	351	7%
Iran	Portugal	345	7%
Spain	Morocco	339	7%
Morocco	Portugal	187	4%
Morocco	Spain	174	3%
Iran	Morocco	141	3%
Morocco	Iran	99	2%

The probability of Iran Advancing, finishing in either of the top two spots in the group, is about 40%. But let's look at what the probability would be if we know Spain isn't getting out. Well then Iran's chances jump up to 67%. If they were independent events knowing something about the outcome, like Spain not getting out, shouldn't alter the probability of the event in question, like Iran getting out. Portugal's chances to advance are 68% but drop to 43% if we are told Morocco will be advancing.

This is just to illustrate that if we think that the odds for Iran to get out of the group are undervalued it'd be likely that we also have the bet for Spain not to get out of the group to be undervalued. This leads to reason that we'll have over valued bets and undervalued bets that are correlated in a group. It seemed as I went through it that most groups there were two teams that were overvalued and two teams that were undervalued.

For each of the eight groups we were essentially making a prediction. For example, in Group B our ideal outcome looked to be Portugal and Iran while in Group F it looked to be Mexico and Sweden, as Germany was overpriced. This was like flipping 8 coins, hoping for heads, but only having educated guesses as to what the probability of a heads is.

Part IV

Friday, da 8th

June 8th, 2018. A day that I thought I may be losing my mind. The end of May saw certain states starting to allow sports betting outside of Las Vegas. I received word that Dover Downs in Delaware was accepting soccer bets compliments of my very thoughtful father. I called Dover Downs to see if the same types of bets that I wanted to place were being offered. They were. Wow. I don't have to fly to Vegas to place these. The tournament starts in less than a week! What should I do?

Now I'll use some time to enlighten you on why on god's green earth was I in this predicament to begin with. Why after spending hundreds of hours on these calculations I was sitting here, less than a week before the World Cup starts, and still not having placed the bets. I had friends that had used Bovada, a sports gambling website, in the past and they didn't seem to have problems with the site. They were only betting like $10 a game though. I was preparing to make over 30 bets and some of the bets being as much as $760. I had, months ago, called Bovada to hammer out the details.

I got information on how the deposits and withdrawals work as well as any other applicable fees. They had said the first deposit was free. There was also a 5.9% deposit fee after the first deposit. Now this part is important as I had explicitly asked them, "So you're telling me if I just make one lump sum deposit I won't get hit with that 5.9% deposit fee?"

"Yes sir, that is correct." The woman said in her Caribbean accent.

While I wouldn't get hit with the deposit fee my bank would charge a 3.5% foreign transaction fee. I had to make sure that made it into my calculations when I was considering what I could be expected to return. They did give me the "free" Bitcoin option but that came with some slight charges of its own not to mention having to worry about the fluctuations in the Bitcoin exchange rate.

The day came where I was actually going to deposit the money. "I'd like to deposit $13,000."

"Wow, sir. Your first deposit can only be up to $1,000."

"What do you mean? $1000? I've asked this multiple times over the last few months. I wanted to make sure I didn't get hit with that 5.9% deposit fee and asked if I just made one big deposit could I avoid this, and they had said yes."

"I'm sorry sir, that was incorrect information." My blood was boiling. You have to be kidding me.

5.9%! I had for a short time considered actually transferring American dollars into euros and then request my girlfriend place the bets for me; there was a bookie less than a minutes walk from her apartment, in Vienna's second district. Despite the proximity to her place I felt like that was a lot to ask as she got quite anxious at the thought of going into those sportsbooks; you know there are a lot of creepy old guys in there. Furthermore, I was calculating that I'd be paying a good amount just in the conversions between US Dollars and Euros. One may pay 3% converting dollars to euros and then would have to pay another 3% going back to dollars when the bets were complete. While it wouldn't be likely the exchange rate would fluctuate dramatically within that month, when my money was locked up in bets, it was a legitimate risk. While I am an actuary I was definitely not in a position to be able to tell how much of a risk it really was and thus led to the decision to avoid it entirely.

I would not recommend using Bovada under any circumstance and I hope the legalization of sports betting here in America makes that crumby company obsolete!

The currency conversions made Bovada more appealing from a purely dollars standpoint. At this point though Bovada started losing some credibility and I got a tad nervous. The employees really don't seem to be on the same page. What's true? What's not? They offered bets which I had made my assumptions off of and could be made from the comfort of my computer. I hadn't really seen these bets offered anywhere else yet and I couldn't get a clear indication if they were being offered in Vegas. I had seen these types of bets in Vegas before but little did I know how hard it would be to find out what the odds were in Vegas from Starbucks in North Carolina. Apparently, one is not allowed to get Vegas sports book odds over the phone. "Can you at least tell me if I can bet for Sweden just to make it out of their group or Serbia not to make it out of their group in the World Cup?" I had asked a Palms sportsbook host.

"Sorry sir, it's against the law."

"Can't you just give me a hint? Is that type of bet offered? You can say frizzle for yes or frazzle for no."

"Sorry sir, I cannot do that. This is being recorded."

"Oy, you're a good employee, take it easy, pull for Sweden!"

My dad used to have a buddy in Henderson, just outside of Vegas, that had been our go to man for circumstances like this. His name was Gary Friedman and he was a highly entertaining and friendly guy. A curly haired, old school, Jew who was the AV guy from high school, who at all times carried around his camera, that never really grew up. This guy was also responsible for getting my brother and myself Superbowl XL tickets in Detroit when the Steelers took on the Seahawks. Unfortunately, Gary had died about a year prior.

My other connection in Vegas happened to be yet another person close to me in my Jewish geography. The cantor for my Bar Mitzvah now resided in Vegas and led one of the Vegas congregations. Go figure but I didn't feel comfortable asking him for help in this case. I decided to throw up some hail mary's on this one. Once again with my slightly loose Jewish connections I sent an email over to the Vegas Moishe House. Moishe House is a Jewish nonprofit organization that tries to connect young adults out of college together. I lived in the Charlotte Moishe House for about a year and a half and had met the Vegas group at the National Convention (think Jew camp for adults) in Wisconsin a summer prior. I offered $200 for someone there to go to some of the casinos to gather all of the spreads for me and report back. But nothing. I couldn't believe it. That Moishe House, I was guessing, must have dissolved for the time being as what kind of Jew is turning down a quick $200.

Well I could just deposit $1000 into Bovada. Perhaps, but I spent all this time on it and I wanted to have a chance at making a lot of money. While I thought I'd be able to update this model relatively easily for conference tournaments in the years to come the thought of missing out on the World Cup tore at me. This only happens every 4 years! Alternatively, I could have different people open accounts and all of us could deposit $1000. This would get us the $13000 of betting interest we desired and we'd avoid that 5.9% fee. At first I thought that idea seemed legitimate but I got worried relying on so many different people to make deposits for me and logistically it was very unappealing.

In the short term I decided to deposit $1000 in the Bovada account, even after being so pissed, and see how it goes. Not particularly well would be the answer. The first day of the deposit seemed fine. $1035 showed up on my online banking account with Bank of America as being taken out of my account and placed into another. Ok that seemed according to plan. It was my $1000 deposit plus the 3.5% foreign transaction fee I had been told about with my bank. The weird thing though is the next day another fee showed up, $36.22. Hmmmmmm. What was this from? Oddly enough I noticed that was 3.5% of the $1035 I had been charged the prior day. It appeared that they had double charged the 3.5%. I mean what the fuck were they trying to pull here? This would spark a couple days of phone tag and he said she said. I called Bovada. They said it was Bank of America charging me but if I decide to call the bank don't mention that they do online gambling. What had I gotten myself into? Should have just gone with my gut to avoid them to begin with. I was just happy I didn't have more money in that account now.

I called Bank of America and they said the $36.22 was their charge and whatever had triggered the 3.5% transaction fee had been from whatever foreign company that made the charge. I tended to believe Bank of America over Bovada. I had been banking with Bank of America roughly 5 years and had no troubles to speak of.

"Dude, I don't give a flying fuck about your policy, I want my money back. I want it out of my account now! And I want you to send me a check now... Like right now." This was me a couple weeks after that initial extra charge talking on the phone with some guy in the Philippines. He was supposedly in charge of all those Caribbean women that I had talked to previously and gotten nowhere. I had finally got it escalated to the big cheese I suppose.

"I understand sir, I will send a check. It should arrive within 20 days. You'll have to go to a bank to deposit it and don't tell them that it's coming from an online gaming source." Shocking. I'm shocked that you'd say that. Ugh!

Great. Fantastic. Lesson learned I say. Thank goodness I didn't go through putting more money in. I probably would have been having a nervous breakdown. A couple weeks later I got a check from a Canadian based telecommunications company. Seriously? I suppose I wasn't even surprised at this point but, in my naivete, I didn't think these things actually happened. What should I be expecting from a sketchy gambling company?

Now fast forward to Friday, June 8th. Off to Dover Downs it is!

I'll drive there I thought. But wait. "There's cheap flights to Philly!" My dad said over the phone.

"Really?"

"Yeah and it looks like it's an hour from Dover."

"Hmmmm, I'll have to see if the banks are open before or after the flights." It was going to be Saturday tomorrow and most of the Bank of America branches were open to 1 at the latest.

At 11:50 pm that night I was still scanning Orbitz and I found a 7:30 am flight from Charlotte to Philadelphia. Holly Ba-Jesus, I'll have to wake up in like four hours. The adrenaline I thought could just keep me up the whole night. Let me see. Ok, I'll get into Philly at like nine, get to a rental car company and have my car by ten. The plan was starting to take shape. Ok, okay...

I checked online for Bank of America branches near Philadelphia and found a big branch in Wilmington, Delaware. Now I had never heard of Wilmington but it looked to be about 30 minutes from the Philly airport and on the way to Dover, and they are open until 1. Ok that leaves me a good cushion to get there before the bank closes but holly shit this is still risky. But like many decisions made in my life, the adrenaline gets pumping and it just happens. Booked! I texted my Jersey friends, Louis and Mike, from undergrad telling them I'd be in the area. They'd be at the Jersey Shore in Long Branch at Mike's parents beach house with another buddy Matt, a cool guy who I had met on a couple of occasions. This could be turning into a fun weekend...

Bat out of Hell

Erur Erur Erur. The alarm clock in my head went off. I rolled over in my bed to my phone on the nightstand. Outside it was still dark and I was up before my actual alarm clock went berserk. Wow, I'm so energized. My body felt sparked. My fingers and my toes and everything else were jolted. This felt like one of those dreams that you don't want to end even though I felt like it had just started. One of the dreams where it felt like you were moving with a purpose and everything just made sense; no one needed to tell me what to do and there was no dead time wondering what to do. I just did.

I carried my one backpack through the Charlotte Douglass airport weaving my way in and out through foot traffic and I was absolutely feeling it. While almost, some would say, dancing to the music in my ears in the airport I was on cloud nine. I was at the gate well in advance of my flight that was scheduled to be on time, fingers crossed. I got out my computer while I waited and looked at the different versions of the model I had generated. I had ones where the momentum factor was bigger, smaller, and excluded all together. I had one where Russia's home field advantage was jacked up about a goal a game. I had one where if teams played teams within their own conference different assumptions took first order. This clean up in the excel workbooks would allow seamless updates. I could update the odds, from Dover Downs, in one workbook and it would flow through all the others. This way I could analyze how good of bargains certain picks were with the new odds under different frameworks. It would then be up to me to blend the different frameworks' findings into my final picks.

I got on the plane where the adrenaline was slightly fading but the couple who sat next to me were quite the chatterboxes. I liked talking to them because they seemed super interested in me. They thought my house hacking idea was clever, thought my background in math and econ was useful, and couldn't really believe that I was flying to Philly to place bets on soccer.

I've always thought of the east coast as lush, as I think the image that comes to mind is the Garden state parkway, but the drive through Delaware was less than awe inspiring. I'm not bashing the Delaware people by any stretch, as I literally had not met a single person from Delaware and I'm sure some would be less than inspired driving through parts of Michigan, but there were lots of open fields here and little to look at. This was probably a good environment for pondering. I found myself doing a lot of that these days. The windows were down, the music was loud, and my backpack was now full of cash. I started thinking about my job and Meine Elena.

Elena

The 2016 European roots trip was where I met my now girlfriend, Elena. I have JSwipe to thank for that. This connection only happened because I was having to slowly expand my search radius for the Jewish females engulfing Krakow. I was just asking people on this dating app to show me around different cities. It was a depressing night in Krakow, following tours and a lot of walking during the day, as the jet lag had finally caught up to me and I was stuck on a couch with little motivation to get up. I was in Krakow and Elena was in Vienna. Although my original plan did not include Vienna, and I was thinking what's the point of this, I kept talking to her. It was pretty spontaneous but after flying to Budapest I got a car, which I inadvertently booked not getting unlimited miles (such a rookie mistake), and drove to Vienna to meet her.

Elena was a brown-eyed and brown-haired beauty with a slight Asian look; I still call her an eskimo child, as did many of the kids growing up with her but most likely not in such a playful manner (hopefully that doesn't offend any of you). Her parents were from what are now Uzbekistan and Tajikistan and grew up in the Soviet Union. I would find out about a year later how old school her mother was in an interrogatory setting utilizing Elena's sister, Hannah, as a Russian-English translator. Elena's mother didn't trust Elena to be an unbiased translator so she called upon Hannah for reinforcements. Her mother allowed Elena to sit at the table with me, albeit in virtual silence. It never crossed my mind that I'd be quizzed on my family's medical history by someone other than a healthcare professional. But that, my friend, is a story for another time.

That first crisp Viennese night, a few hours after arriving in Budapest, I met Elena at Chilai, a nice coffee shop in first district near the city center. She didn't really spend much time with me, maybe for my own tardiness, and she asked me direct questions. Very direct questions.

Sitting at the booth a slight pause came and then, "You know, can I ask you a question?" I could barely hear an accent on this girl. Countries outside the US must think we're such dumb people, virtually all of us only know one language, and some of us barely one.

"What if I say no?"

"Have you ever done drugs?" So much for her caring about how I replied. I was taken aback I have to say. Most girls beat around the bush but not Elena. This girl was all business.

"Ummm, I tried marijuana after one of our fraternity soccer wins but didn't really feel anything."

Are your shoes Vans (she seemed abnormally interested when asking this question)? Why are you here? Why did you lose your job? Why were you creepy and ask me to show you around the city in your car (She may have only mentioned this creepiness later on but I'm 90% sure she asked something related)? The questions went on and on, and while the information exchange was quite lopsided, I was able to gain some information about her.

She recently started working for one of the agencies at the UN on a six-month contract job. She had dragged out her undergrad while working at Austrian Airlines and in the process became very well-traveled. She took Japanese at Uni, as all the Viennese call it, and had been to Japan a couple times and to Singapore with her dad. She was a city girl through and through. She liked taking the subway to and fro and very much enjoyed earning money to support her dining out habits. I could totally relate to and appreciate this.

She was ready to part ways after my small plate of pasta and some tea. As we were walking out I realized I still didn't know how to pronounce her name, "wait how do you pronounce your name?"

"It's El-Eh-Nah."

Christmas Eve, the following day, she had me into her dad's bar after I had strolled through, yet another, old art museum in the Belvedere on her recommendation. She occasionally worked at her dad's bar, which was cleverly called Jakov's. Her dad was what I envisioned my dad's dad to be like. An olive-skinned man that walked slowly, kind of dragging his feet along, and took a puff of his cigarette every step or at least every other. The bar was named after him, Jakov. Did I mention that? Jakov is my Hebrew name, translates to Jacob, and thus we had an instant connection (well we probably would have if he spoke any English or if I spoke some German, I'm positive of this). By instant connection I mean just on my end as I couldn't understand a lick of what he was saying. I believe it not to be particularly friendly. Throughout the bar period I wasn't sure if I was happy or jealous I didn't know German as I could only guess what they were saying around me and possibly about me. *What are there no women in America? Who comes to Austria not knowing a lick of German? Stupid American.* I did once attempt to tell Jakov, in German as Elena had trained me, that the food was great but he looked at me with a blank stare. I could tell in his mind he was shaking his head very slowly left to right and thinking, "gosh this kid."

The self-naming didn't belie the interior of the bar. There were 4 stools at the bar and some seating against the walls which were lined with pictures of Jakov. There's one picture in particular that sticks out in my mind. It was a picture of him in a purple jersey which is what the local football team, F.K. Austria Vienna, wore. Their dog Chuck, a big trained killing machine of a Belgium shepherd, who scared the life out of me made many appearances along the walls. I was just happy that beast wasn't here. Many months later when I'd eventually meet Chuck I was equally happy that he was wearing a muzzle at all times. What an animal. I will say Chucky (see I call him Chucky now) has grown on me and I enjoy saying the commands in German, "Sitz, platz, Tsu mir, Frei."

Elena totally could run the bar solo. She knew everyone that came through the doors and everyone knew her. She authoritatively stood behind the bar manning the cappuccino machine, slight smokers fog mudding my view, and pouring lots of wine for a midday; it is 10 pm somewhere I've been told. They had the yummiest of yummy pastas and I joked that the pasta was the most likely thing to bring me back to this city. Around noon my Christmas Eve with Elena was over and I was off to Bratislava. Driving away I actually thought there was a high probability I'd never see that girl again. I could tell quickly she was made differently but we were on different continents and that couldn't possibly work. Right? While many would say my lifestyle and personality was growing towards a European's, as my fondness for soccer seemed to trump every other aspect of my life, I will strongly say I do love America. Little did I know Elena would become a big part of my life.

The Bratislava malarkey, following Vienna, consisted of a lonely Christmas Eve walking around the downtown seeing the communist relics and poking my head inside the occasional church to help remind myself that there were, indeed, people alive. The zombie apocalypse hadn't begun quite just yet, even though I can't say I saw one smile in that country. The memorable part of that Bratislava stint, that really only lasted like 4 hours, was when I was walking back to my car.

I mean when you have to go you have to go, right? I did what any other guy would do. While Bratislava was a completely decent city and not in any way nestled away in the woods I did think I'd be fine taking a pee behind a gas station. I mean there were no people walking around, as everyone was in church if they were out of their homes, and I saw no churches in close proximity. Keep in mind I had to go bad, this was not just a little tinkle but a big tinkle.

When I started I immediately felt relief. There's no way I would have made it back to my car and found an open gas station or truck stop. And then mid pee came.

I looked up and a car was taking a sharp turn towards me. What the hell? Where'd that thing come from? This was happening in fractions of a second. Is that a stump on the top of the car? I felt like the Slovakian law torpedo was heading right at me. Cops? Seriously? I wouldn't fare well in a Slovakian cell.

I took a few steps back, mid streaming, and thought do I really want to find out if that's really the police? I kept back tracking and then just had to pull my pants up, did a 180-degree turn, and shot off to a park a tad behind the gas station that had some decent cover and dropped amongst the shrubbery. I peered up to see the passing car. Gosh, I can't even tell if that's a cop car. My heart was beating fast and was the only thing I could hear. My pants were wet and I felt defeated, or better said pounded, by the Slovakian people. I was straddling the base of a bush in the heart of Bratislava, looking up into the dreary sky, had not been given one smile, had just wet my pants as a 27-year-old, and now felt a snow flake hit my cheek. Just get me to Budapest.

Part V

Dover Downs

I finally got to the exit for Dover. The ominous clouds were percolating towards us and rain seemed imminent. Dover was basically a single street going in and out of the city as far as I could tell, not what I would have thought for a state capital, and made for easy navigation. Looking back, I didn't see the capital building and, more surprisingly, hadn't wondered where it was. I did however pass a bunch of chain restaurants. Panda Express, Chicka-fil-a, and Qdoba all sounded like good lunch options to look over the odds once I picked them up at the sportsbook. I drove for another 5 minutes and on my left was Dover Downs.

I thought this was just a racetrack but there was also an elegant yet dominant looking hotel, probably 8 to 10 stories tall, attached. Back and to the left one could see that a monstrous stadium lay there. I'm guessing that was where people went to watch the ponies and probably where the sportsbook is located. A big sign directing me, not shockingly, back and to the left of this structure stood at the entrance directing me to the sportsbook. Voila!

Man-o-man was I excited; total adrenaline was pumping through me once again. How am I this awake when I got up so early with such little sleep? The crash was coming right? While I never officially pulled an all-nighter in college I came close, thanks to Psychology 111, and this feeling was like that. I just had to keep this up a bit longer before I could crash.

It was oddly enough the day of the Preakness. In American thoroughbred horse racing there are three big races, which if a horse wins all of them is referred to as winning the Triple Crown. One is the Kentucky Derby which is held in Louisville, one is Belmont which is held in New York, and one is the Preakness which is held in Baltimore. I heard someone say that it's only for three-year-old thoroughbred horses. And while I'd consider myself a slight believer in Karma I could only see this as a good sign. Threes were showing up all over the place and my longest lasting soccer number was the number three. The stars were aligning for the good guys!

While it was good on the karma front it wasn't ideal for my anxiety level. I was thinking there would be a tremendous number of people placing bets. One, I didn't want to have to wait long to place the bets and two, I didn't want people getting annoyed with me placing so many bets, maybe more than 30. Just imagine this old kid at the bookie desk with wads of cash fumbling through the green placing bet after bet. Luckily on this mission I was not placing any bets.

This penetrating mission was solely to gather my sheets for soccer bets. I walked through the sports books and marched to the left side of the betting desks where all the betting sheets were housed. There they were, fresh off the presses. We'd be some of the first Americans to place sports bets outside of Las Vegas, legally at least. I believe a famous man was once quoted as saying, "one small step for man, one giant leap for mankind."

I picked up three sheets. One was the sheet that a large majority of our bets would come from and eventually $7,780 of our $8,010 would be spent on these types of bets. They were the bets for each team just to get out of their group and the bets for teams to not get out of their respective groups. Once again, the format goes like this, eight groups of four, everyone plays everyone else in the group resulting in 6 games played amongst all the teams.

1. Team 1 plays Team 2
2. Team 1 plays Team 3
3. Team 1 plays Team 4
4. Team 2 plays Team 3
5. Team 2 plays Team 4
6. Team 3 plays Team 4

A win gets a team 3 points and a tie gets each team 1 point while a loss punishes you with 0 points. The 2 teams with the most points, along with other tiebreaking procedures, advance to the knockout stage of the tournament while the other two will have to wait another 4 years, maybe longer, to have another crack at the World Cup. So why would most of our money be put in this type of bet? Although a sample size of 3 is not a lot and would lack credibility towards reaching any real conclusions in any normal statistical setting it was still better than betting on just one game. One thing that soccer is great for is the brutal game where one team dominates but can't put it in the net and the other team gets a fortunate goal going the other way.

Based off the preliminary odds from Bovada Switzerland was one of our highest ranked bets. This was not because we thought they were the most likely team to get out of their group but because we thought they had a good chance of getting out and the odds being offered, given our estimated probability, were a bargain in our eyes. We had them getting out of Group E between 60-65% of the time, depending on the specific coefficients we were using for a particular model, and Bovada had them at -105 (one would have to bet $1.05 to make an additional $1). For ease sake let's assume 60% of the time Switzerland would get out of Group E which consists of Brazil, Switzerland, Serbia, and Costa Rica (Brazil being a heavy favorite with the other slot kind of up for grabs). That's 3/5 of the time so for every 3 successes there'd be 2 losses. A risk neutral person would be willing to pay $3 to win an additional $2. On Bovada we would have only had to have put $2.10 to win $2. In our eyes that was a cheap bet because we're saying we'd be willing to pay $3 and the bookies are only charging us $2.10 for every $2 that we'd like to win! The Dover Downs line for Switzerland was listed at +105, even better! Now to win $2 we wouldn't even have to bet $2, it got cheaper!

WILL SWITZERLAND ADVANCE FROM GROUP E

TV TIME	BET #	PROPOSITION	M/L
	8539	YES	+105
8:00 AM	8540	NO	-125

The second sheet was the overall champion sheet with defending champions, Germany, at the top of the sheet at 3 to 1 followed closely by Brazil at 7 to 2. Panama, not shown below, and Saudi Arabia were viewed as the worst of the pack for winning it all coming in at 750 to 1. These lines were essentially hot off the press as could be seen from the "Odds as of 06/05/18" in the rightmost column. All odds on this sheet remained unchanged since the start of the week. That wasn't all that surprising considering that months ago I already had the odds on Bovada. Betters have had some time to start placing bets and things appear to have stabilized and found an equilibrium. It was only a week out from the start of the tournament.

BET #	TEAMS	OPENING ODDS	ODDS AS OF 6/05/18
99001	Germany	3/1	3/1
99002	Argentina	5/1	5/1
99003	Spain	11/2	11/2
99004	France	11/2	11/2
99005	Brazil	7/2	7/2

99006	Belgium	8/1	8/1
99007	England	16/1	16/1
99008	Portugal	18/1	18/1
...			
99014	Switzerland	90/1	90/1
99015	Poland	40/1	40/1
...			
99030	Tunisia	600/1	600/1
99031	Iran	300/1	300/1
99032	Saudi Arabia	750/1	750/1

The third sheet was the champions of each group. Hmmm, I thought. I remembered when I did my initial analysis the few bets we'd make for teams to win their respective groups were Portugal, Peru, and Switzerland albeit at much lower dollar amounts than teams just advancing or not advancing from their groups.

Portugal won the European championship a mere two years ago, with arguably the best player in the world in Cristiano Ronaldo, and still look to be getting little respect in Group B. Undefeated in their last two years of qualifying games in Europe Portugal was listed at +180 (if one bets a dollar and Portugal wins the group they'd get their original $1 back plus another $1.80) while Spain was listed as the favorite at -200 (one would need to bet $2 to get their original $2 plus $1). That means betters are essentially giving Portugal a 36% chance of winning their group. We'll be betting on that as the odds are unchanged since I got the Bovada odds months ago. It actually appeared even more people had jumped on the Spanish bandwagon. I had originally seen Spain at -190 and it was now at -200 (meaning you have to put more money down than before to win a dollar).

TO WIN GROUP B

Friday, June 15, 2018

Bet #	Teams	Odds as of 06/05/18
99056	SPAIN	-200
99057	PORTUGAL	+180
99058	MOROCCO	+1600
99059	IRAN	+3000

I was one of those kids looking straight down at the sheets as I made my exit from the sportsbook, much like the kids that would read those science fiction books through the halls of high school that used to annoy me ever so much. Couldn't they do that some other time? I'm not even sure if I took time to say excuse me as I zoned out and floated across sportsbook carpet. Moving ever so slowly amongst the Preakness crowd it started to hit me. Wait what was hitting me? I was so tired I was having trouble concentrating now. The runner's high or in my case the potential better's high was fading fast. I plopped down in the car, sheets in lap, and dozed off for a bit.

Time to Analyze... More (Fucking Sergio Ramos Causing Me Problems Again)

What seemed like an eternity was a mere fifteen minutes. A fifteen minutes that did not really reinvigorate me but left me reclined with drool sliding down the left side of my cheek while the raindrops were plopping down outside. Ah, there's work to be done! I looked down at my phone and saw a text from Louis asking on my time of arrival. That seemed very far in the distance. I needed to go chart out my bets, come back and place them, and then drive about three hours north to the Jersey Shore to meet Louis and the guys. And I think I need some food... Like pronto.

Chick-Fil-A seemed to be the logical selection for lunch. Obviously because I was now living in Charlotte, NC where there are Chick-Fil-A's a plenty and I never go to any of them. But the Chick-Fil-A here seemed more off beat and I thought it would make for good munchie food while I scanned the odds sheets; the sheets controlled by my left hand and the chicken sandwich controlled by my right. I was just going to do a cursory check to see how these odds differed from my original odds that I had acquired from Bovada a few months prior. These I had scribbled in my very handy light green, tree of life, notebook, and had been the framework of which I had come up with my preliminary bets. I was thinking they wouldn't have changed much. The analysis continued from Chick-Fil-A to the Starbucks down the road as the sky got closer and closer to total downpour.

Simply put the odds did not really change that much. I sat at Starbucks for about 4 hours, sipping on my usual green tea Frappuccino with my noise canceling construction earmuffs, going through different allocations of the betting money. While I had looked at this many times I was now concerned about my initial distribution of the money by group. While I had set limits before by team, 10% of the total money bet which may have been crazy to begin with, when everything was in aggregate a slightly different picture had taken shape. There were much better deals in certain groups which lead to much more money being bet on a few select groups which gave me the feeling of putting all my eggs in a couple of baskets. Furthermore, it started feeling really like I was essentially making eight different bets, that were not necessarily all or nothing bets, even though I'd be placing over 30. Like I said before while this method is all great in theory, bet on the best deals duh, when I actually had to finalize the dollar amounts and realized there were real financial impacts to these decisions, while exciting, was also nerve wracking.

I actually realized also that managing other people's money was also different than managing mine alone. If it had just been my money on the line I'm not sure I would have checked and re-checked so many of my numbers, assumptions, and projections. I found myself rechecking certain stats and how using the different variable coefficients affected the betting amounts.

A Is for up in the Air

I originally had Egypt as very undervalued in the, what appeared to be, very weak Group A. It consisted of hosts Russia, Uruguay, and Saudi Arabia. Mohammed Salah, Egypt's best player, and arguably best player on the planet for the last 6 months, had just been hurt a couple weeks ago in their Champions League Final against Cristiano Ronaldo's Real Madrid. On the play central defender Sergio Ramos, master of the dark arts as many refer to him, pulled a play out of a wrestling book. While maybe a slight exaggeration the result was a separated shoulder for Salah which now had him in doubt for this tournament. Salah plays his club football at Liverpool in England and the reports were coming out of England saying that he could miss up to two games even though the Egyptian Football Association was saying Salah was up and running well. I was hesitant now to bet big money on Egypt because so much of their team was dependent on how Salah performed and quite frankly I believed the English reports more than the Egyptian ones. And then I started questioning Russia more in that very same group.

I mean what was Russia's real home field advantage? How was I to really know? They had played very few competitive games since the last World Cup and they were years ago. I had done sensitivity testing on this consisting of tinkering with Russia's home field advantage. I saw that Russia would require a whole extra goal of predicted goal differential added on to their original home field advantage assumption to make Egypt's odds to get out of the group start looking ordinary. The original home field advantage assumption was .3 goals against European teams and .4 goals against non-European teams. This was based off the home field advantage analysis I had done prior but really wasn't specific to Russia so much as it was a European conference assumption.

Egypt had started out as one of my top picks. The current odds suggested many others also thought that they were undervalued. The original Bovada line for Egypt to get out of the group was +160 and now it was just +125. I still liked Egypt but didn't like them quite as much at that payout. We would be getting back 35 cents less per dollar bet if we were to win. The risk reward had taken a hit, and while initially I could have seen why, I questioned if it had gotten even lower before Salah got hurt. With a healthy Mo Salah that +160 seemed like a steal! +125, while still good, was not quite as good.

The unknown around Russia's home field advantage assumption, Egypt's lessened payout, and capped off with the questionability of Mo Salah's availability, caused me to lower the Egypt bet to $320 from about $600. I also lowered the bet of Russia not getting out of the group to $400 even though it was still at +235 and we had them not getting out about 60% of the time. It was rare for a home team to not advance from the group stage but then again not many hosts had been as lowly ranked as Russia (ranked 65th in the FIFA standings entering the tournament).

It was likely Uruguay would get out of Group A; I had them getting out about three quarters of the time while Vegas had them slightly higher at 83%. Our total exposure to Group A ended up being $760, much lower than initially projected, as we also placed a small bet on Saudi Arabia to get out at +1200. The return probabilities are in the scatterplot below. Much would hinge on Russia's performance. We just needed them to not get out!

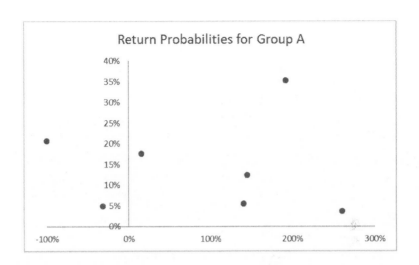

Return Probabilities for Group A

E Is for Excellent

While Group A's total dollar bet was relatively small two of my top 4 bets of the whole tournament were coming from Group E. They both looked to be great bargains. We thought Switzerland was underrated and Serbia was grossly overrated. My top bet, at $760 bet, for Switzerland to get out of the group would collect $1520 if they did. My fourth highest dollar bet, also from Group E, was a bet of $580 for Serbia not to get out of the group and would collect $994 if they failed to get out of the group. The thing was they were both in Brazil's group. I thought to myself, but Brazil like always gets out of the group! It was likely we would win both or lose both, about a 70% chance I was calculating.

Costa Rica seemed like the step child that no one cared about as they were the fourth team in Group E. This was despite them getting to the quarterfinals in Brazil 2014 and the fact they were spear headed by the phenomenal Real Madrid goal keeper, Keylor Navas. I also put a $220 bet on Costa Rica to advance at +425. Our total bets on Group E ended up being $1,630. The returns are in the scatterplot below.

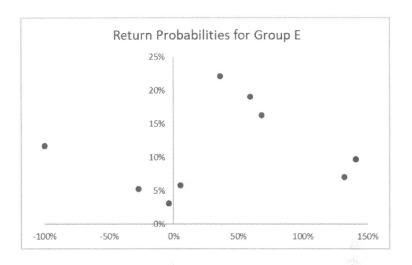

Despite the FIFA ranking progression below Switzerland's main competition for a spot in the knock out round in Group E was Serbia, according to the bookies. Those old Yugoslavian countries always scare me because they truly are fantastic at ball sports. It sounds cliché but they are better than the sum of their parts. Considering their population, I would say collectively they are the best in the world. Serbia had some intriguing players that play in the top leagues in the world like Nemanja Matic at Manchester United and Sergej Milinkovic-Savic for Lazio, who was now being linked with a move to Real Madrid at just 23 years old.

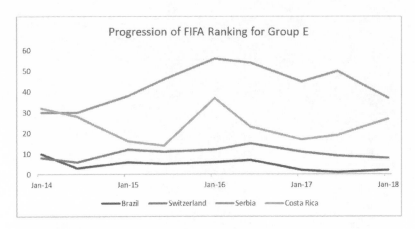

Switzerland was damn good though too I reminded myself. They had only lost one meaningful game in the past two years, away to Portugal, and were currently 6th in the world FIFA rankings. Just look at how smooth their line is above; it does show consistency against the teams they have played. While my model was fully driven from current FIFA rankings and shifts in the FIFA rankings (I referred to these as the momentum shift) I was starting to get antsy as if I may have missed some important variables.

Would the player salaries have given me a different result on this matchup? On paper Serbia looked pretty good. Although they had the fewest points of any of the nine qualifying group winners, at 21, they still won and held off the likes of Ireland, Wales, and Austria. After all of that though they were still the lowest ranked team in Europe outside of Russia, entering the tournament at 38 in the world. I only had them getting out of the group about a quarter of the time.

It is one thing to say you like a bet but then when it really comes to putting your money on how confident you are you really start to scrutinize lots of information and reasonings behind your feelings. In the chart above one would say we had predicted about an 80% chance of at least getting our money back but there is still that pesky 20%. The doomsday outcome would be if Brazil and Serbia advanced; we would lose everything.

B Is for Boring

While Switzerland in Group E was undervalued and, according to our probabilities, expected to get out of the group I did not have that luxury with some of the other groups. For example, in Group B Spain and Portugal were heavily favored to get out of the group that also had Iran and Morocco. The odds made it in such a way that we were chasing the hope that Iran could sneak out of that group.

I did not want to risk lots of money on Spain or Portugal to just get out of the group. One would have had to lay lots of money to bet on them, -1600 in Spain's case and -410 in Portugal's. You read that correct, one would have to lay 16 dollars on Spain just to make 1 dollar to get out of the group. The modeling suggested Iran would get out about 30% of the time and the odds were at +600. Morocco's odds seemed right in line with what my model had so we did not bet on them to make it out or to not make it out. Gosh that would be unbelievable if Iran could knock out Spain or Portugal!

Portugal, as the top team in that group according to the FIFA rankings, seemed undervalued, at +180, to outright win the group as Spain was now priced at -200 to win Group B which was grossly overpriced in my eyes. Group B's returns looked like the below and you will notice there's a much higher probability of us losing money in this group, almost 50%. If Iran could find a way through the returns would be tremendous. Due to the added probability of losing I only bet $370 on group B, $200 of it being on Iran getting out of the group.

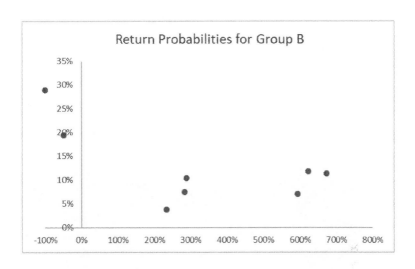

F Is for Frenetically Fantastic

When I initially went through my analysis this was the most stellar group in my eyes, basically due to the high probability of at least getting our money back. Group F was comprised of the former World Champions Germany, Mexico, South Korea, and the pesky Swedes who knocked out Italy to qualify. This group had a couple dynamics that were playing out that made things favorable I believe.

This was the only group where there were two teams we had getting out between 50% - 60% of the time and which came with favorable odds. Those teams were Mexico and Sweden, at -115 and +140 respectively. Basically, I went into this group viewing it as a hedge group. You will see in the return probabilities for Group F that there was an incredibly high probability of us at least getting our money back on this group; almost 90%! If the group went as expected with Germany and Mexico we'd basically get our money back and if there was a way that Sweden could sneak in that would just be gravy.

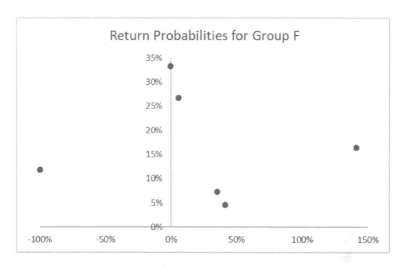

Return Probabilities for Group F

Vegas had Korea not getting out of the group at about 83%, at -475. We saw that as pretty fair or even slightly underpriced. The reason Sweden and Mexico appeared to be such bargains stemmed from the fact many people were betting on Germany getting out of the group, similar to the Spain group except this time there appeared to be two teams capable of getting out and not just one like in Spain's group with Portugal. Germany was listed to get out of the group at -1450, translating to almost 95%. We had them getting out about 75% of the time, meaning we thought it should only be about -300. On the flip side one could bet for Germany not to get out of the group at +1000. I felt kind of dumb doing this, as I basically had mentally penciled Germany through, but decided to bet $60 on Germany not to get out at +1000; if that craziness were to happen I would get my $60 plus another $600. Our doomsday scenario here was if Germany and South Korea were to advance but we only viewed that happening about 12% of the time. The other combinations would basically fund the initial investment and offer the possibility of a big payday. We bet $1180 on this group, our third largest dollar amount of any one group, comprising mostly on Sweden and Mexico getting out.

H Is for Potential Hell

I am going to start this discussion with the return probability chart for Group H consisting of Poland, Colombia, Senegal, and Japan:

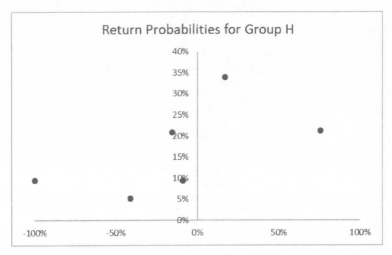

One can see, similar to Group B, we have a fairly high probability of losing money in this group, about 45%. With this in mind one may think that we chose to bet little in this case, and in retrospect maybe we should have as you can also see that only two of the possible six permutations lead to positive results. Now unlike betting on an underdog in B, where we bet on Iran, I thought Group H had, not great, but slight bargains in what we were viewing as likely outcomes in Poland advancing and Japan not advancing. Remember Poland was in bucket 1 when the draw occurred meaning they were one of the top 7 ranked teams in the world going into the tournament. They had a rare opportunistic goal scoring machine in Bayern Munich's Robert Lewandowski who had scored more goals than anyone in European qualifying, with sixteen, while averaging a goal every 56 minutes of playing.

Unlike an underdog, like with Iran in Group B, where you don't have to lay a lot of money to collect a good chunk of change Group H did not provide that luxury. Poland was at -155 to get out of the group and Japan was at -270 to not get out of the group. We would have to give up good chunks of change, but nothing like in Group B with Spain and Portugal, to make money in this group. We also placed smaller bets on Senegal getting out and Colombia not getting out. We ended up putting $1,470 on bets in this group, our second largest dollar group. We would lose everything if Colombia and Japan advanced and left no room for profits if Japan were to get out, even if Poland also advanced. This was the only group where we were so dependent on the performance of one team, and it came from the fact that we were laying $500 on Japan not advancing at -270.

Looking Past the Group Stage

While our bread and butter would be made on the teams in the group stage we also threw up some higher flyers on who would win the whole shebang. We placed $10 bets on Portugal, Switzerland, and Poland to win it all at the odds below with the exception of Portugal that dropped to +1500 from +1800. While our analysis thought the usual suspects were all overpriced we still had each of Brazil and France winning it all about 7% of the time and decided to lay $40 on each of them at +350 and +550 respectively. This was the only time in this process where we bet on what we considered overpriced bets from every which way we looked at it.

BET #	TEAMS	OPENING ODDS	ODDS AS OF 6/05/18
99001	Germany	3/1	3/1
99002	Argentina	5/1	5/1
99003	Spain	11/2	11/2
99004	France	11/2	11/2
99005	Brazil	7/2	7/2
99006	Belgium	8/1	8/1
99007	England	16/1	16/1
99008	Portugal	18/1	18/1
...			
99014	Switzerland	90/1	90/1
99015	Poland	40/1	40/1
...			
99030	Tunisia	600/1	600/1
99031	Iran	300/1	300/1
99032	Saudi Arabia	750/1	750/1

Part VI

My Triple Crown

All great things come in threes, right? It was once again karma playing a role in this process. While the Preakness was going on I would be placing $8,010 over 34 different bets. I had a sheet with my amounts and bet numbers handy and had decided, as I was once again scared of carrying tons of money at once, I would be making three separate trips into Dover Downs.

I had an almost comical vision in my mind's eye of me walking through the parking lot towards the sportsbook entrance and getting sucker punched in my right cheek bone. I was in shock. In slow motion and absolutely no sound to speak of, my left foot slips to the right on the wet pavement and my body makes its way to the horizontal. It gets worse. The money in my kangaroo pouch shoots up in the air like old faithful, falls majestically in the perpetrator's hands, and he would walk away in anonymity with me lying there in the parking lot crying like a little kid. All that money to never be seen again.

It was this image that triggered me to take the three separate trips inside. There actually was not that long of a line for the counter. They had set up machines to accommodate horse race bets which were very much occupied but the line to the counter was non-existent. When I got to the counter and pulled the big wad of cash out I immediately felt like all eyes were on me. I looked around. There were no eyes on me. Ok, I'm in peace. I started going down the list and reading the counter lady off the bet numbers and amounts. After I told her each bet she would read off the current odds and confirm the bet. By and large there were not significant fluctuations between the odds I had picked up earlier this afternoon and what she was reciting to me. As I got down the list I noticed a line forming behind me. I heard someone behind say, "this kid is fucking crazy."

I had just dropped about 3 thousand in bets. After confirming the money was correct the counter lady said, "Good luck."

"I'll be back in soon. I just need to go get more money." She could not have cared less that I would soon be back to see her. I took my tickets, shoved them in my poach, and walked out to the car.

I did this two more times. Each trip to the car involved me putting the newly received tickets in my backpack and locking that backpack in the trunk. A crazy thing happened to me right after I placed my third round of bets; I shit you not. This guy, who was peering at me while I was placing the bets, came up to me after I took the tickets. He asked, "what should I bet on?"

"What type of bet are you looking for?"

"I don't care. I'm about to go away next week."

"What do you mean?"

"Like I'm about to go to prison for a while. I don't care. What should I bet on?"

Wow this took me aback. This dude had touched me on my arm like we had been pals forever. I did not know his name. I did not know his story. I did not want to know his story and I definitely was not his pal. "Well my biggest bet I placed was Switzerland to get out of their group. I just put $760 on them. I really think it's a solid bet. They're at even money."

"Thanks." And that was that. The bets were placed.

| Type | Country | Vegas | | Betting Budget | If win | Group |
		To win - Vegas	Pay - Vegas	8,010		
Adv.Gr	Switzerland	100	100	760	1,520	E
Adv.Gr	Peru	170	100	700	1,890	C
Adv.Gr	Poland	100	155	620	1,020	H
No.Adv.Gr	Serbia	100	140	580	994	E
Adv.Gr	Iceland	280	100	560	2,128	D
Adv.Gr	Tunisia	450	100	560	3,080	G
Adv.Gr	Mexico	100	115	500	935	F
No.Adv.Gr	Japan	100	270	500	685	H
Adv.Gr	Sweden	140	100	420	1,008	F
No.Adv.Gr	Russia	235	100	400	1,340	A
Adv.Gr	Egypt	175	100	320	880	A
Adv.Gr	Senegal	130	100	240	552	H
Adv.Gr	Costa Rica	425	100	220	1,155	E
Adv.Gr	Iran	600	100	200	1,400	B
No.Adv.Gr	South Korea	100	475	200	242	F
No.Adv.Gr	Nigeria	100	290	180	242	D
No.Adv.Gr	Denmark	120	100	120	264	C
No.Adv.Gr	France	1,100	100	100	1,200	C
No.Adv.Gr	England	500	100	100	600	G
No.Adv.Gr	Spain	1,100	100	100	1,200	B
No.Adv.Gr	Argentina	450	100	100	550	D
No.Adv.Gr	Colombia	210	100	100	310	H
No.Adv.Gr	Croatia	185	100	60	171	D
No.Adv.Gr	Germany	1,000	100	60	660	F
Win.Gr	Portugal	200	100	60	180	B
Win.Gr	Peru	850	100	40	380	C
Adv.Gr	Saudi Arabia	1,200	100	40	520	A
No.Adv.Gr	Belgium	800	100	40	360	G
Win.WC	France	550	100	40	260	C
Win.WC	Brazil	350	100	40	180	E
Win.Gr	Switzerland	600	100	20	140	E
Win.WC	Switzerland	9,000	100	10	910	E
Win.WC	Poland	4,000	100	10	410	H
Win.WC	Portugal	1,500	100	10	160	B

Key

Type Code	Type of Bet
Adv.Gr	Advance from group
No.Adv.Gr	Not to advance from group
Win.Gr	Win group
Win.WC	Win World Cup

Da Shore

The bets were placed. I had all 34 tickets and they were not leaving my tight white jean shorts pocket. I thought I would feel more accomplishment. I mean I felt a slight satisfaction, and more than anything a great sense of relief, but it was accompanied by a persistent tingling anxiety. All I could do now was wait and watch. Luckily it was just a week away. Regardless of the outcome I would be happy of the decision to come here and place the bets. After all, if not for that decision I would not be writing to you now.

It was almost six o'clock in the evening and the Louis text messages continued to inquire what the hell was taking me so long. I tried explaining this process could not be rushed, I had to take my time! It would take about three hours to get to Mike's place in Long Branch up on the Jersey Shore.

There is this restaurant along the shore called Rooney's. The place has great food and even has an iconic doggy water bowl along the ocean side trail for the thirsty dogs that have over ambitious owners. We had been there once before and Louis had said the plan was to get a late dinner there. It sure would be late but telling the guys about all the bets excited me. I was thinking they would be optimistically skeptical of my endeavor. I sometimes think I am crazy myself. I not once used a single player's stats to feed my model and still bet eight grand. I landed in Philly this morning and would be heading back to Philly tomorrow to catch my flight home. What a whirlwind.

After a great Rooney's dinner, a lot of Lil Dickey music videos accompanied with vintage Mike dance moves, classic Amy's breakfast food with Louis while the others were too "tired" to get up, and a glow in the dark golf outing that ended in victory it was time to make my way back to Charlotte. This was a story on its own.

Remember I had booked this flight on Friday; that was just two days prior. I booked this flight so late that there were no direct flights to Charlotte. I had to fly through D.C. on the way back. Last time I flew to Jersey on United I had about ten hours wasted from non-weather delays. This time it was more of the same. A couple of delays and next thing I knew I was sleeping on the floor in the Dulles airport protecting my betting tickets like it was my lifeline. I did manage to crack open a celebratory Coke and watch some NetFlix while lying on the airport floor in peace and quiet. I was scheduled to be at work tomorrow but it was now looking like I would miss the morning at a minimum. What a weekend I kept telling myself. Theoretically I could be doing adventures like this every weekend. Maybe I should but I probably should plan a bit further in advance so I don't pay an arm and a leg.

Shocker shocker. I missed the morning at work. I took a Lyft from the airport home, took a quick shower, and then made my way to work. I was essentially a walking zombie at this point around lunch time. I walked slowly through the office, said hi to my boss at the cubicle directly next to me, and made like it was just some other weekend I was coming back from. This had been anything but an ordinary weekend and it was one I will remember for the rest of my life. I hope to tell this story to my children one day. Hopefully they will say that it was super cool that I decided to go to Delaware and then hang with my buddies for a day or they may just be like, 'damn, you crazy pops.' My life may be relatively boring the next few days; there is only so much excitement a spreadsheet can provide... a work spreadsheet that is.

Part VII

Week One

Week One of the tournament was a topsy turvy show as unexpected things have a tendency of showing themselves early on. It started off with a bang as Russia crushed Saudi Arabia 5-0 in a game where the model only had Russia favored by .3 goals and about a 70% of either winning or tying. I thought my home field advantage assumption may have been slightly underestimated. Time will tell.

There was the tragedy of Peru totally outplaying Denmark but losing 1-0 to an impressive showing by Danish goalkeeper Kasper Schmeichel and to a failed penalty kick by Christian Cueva. Peru was in a pickle and so were our Group C bets. We had bet $700, our second largest dollar bet, on Peru to advance and a smaller bet on Denmark not to advance. This was a double whammy and we looked bleak to return from this result. They were in France's group after all.

During the World Cup every morning was spent watching the World Cup. On the weekends it was easier and on one of the days I remember squirming in a lounge chair at Starbucks as Iceland was defending for their lives against Messi's Argentina. After a missed penalty kick, by no other than Lionel Messi, against all odds, Iceland, a nation of roughly three hundred and thirty thousand people, tied one of the juggernauts in world football 1-1.

Week Two

Week two of the tournament, once again sitting at my cubicle in my office, I had my phone streaming the Switzerland Serbia game, my boss in the next cube mind you. Two of our largest bets strongly hinged on the outcome of this game. We wanted Switzerland to advance and we did not want Serbia to advance. Serbia was up 1-0, compliments of a fifth minute Mitrovic goal, and my heart was beating out of my chest. I felt physically ill. Switzerland was playing well per their usual methodical ways. They should be winning I thought. While Switzerland had played phenomenally well in their first match and pulled off an unexpected tie versus Brazil if Serbia were to beat Switzerland today, as Serbia had beaten Costa Rica in their first match, Serbia would be through and we could kiss our $1,630 goodbye for Group E. Then something magical happened.

In the 53rd minute a left-footed bomb from deep, by no other than the Arsenal man Granit Xhaka, tied the game. My fists smashed my desk. I looked over to my boss in a slow 90 degree turn hands opening to the ceiling, "dumb spreadsheet."

Inside I was going nuts. I normally complained about Xhaka when he played for Arsenal but right now I would have been smothering him with kisses. Oh, my goodness! I have never felt relief like that before in my life and that is not an exaggeration. Switzerland was still alive! Our bet was still alive! Our money was still alive! And then the unthinkable happened.

A man that was born in Kosovo, a piece of land that Serbia claims to have rights to, that immigrated with his family to

Switzerland and played on the Swiss national team, had a chance with just him and the Serbian goal keeper in the 90th minute. Xherdan Shaqiri, the small pesky winger, slotted home a winner that sent the Swiss faithful into euphoria and a goal that appeared to mean so much more to him as a person. Adrenaline was pumping and I was so happy I felt a tear coming on. This meant a Swiss tie against Costa Rica in the next match would be enough for Switzerland to advance. Serbia would need to beat Brazil to have a chance. While I had not thought of the guy that was going to prison, since speaking with him at Dover Downs, I wondered if he put the money he had on Switzerland. Was he now a Swiss fan for life? Now I wondered.

Week Three

Week three is decision week. It is the week that would define many teams' legacies in this tournament and would chart out how the knock out rounds could play out. While Poland had already been eliminated, along with the majority of our bets, it was still must see tv and I could not get enough of it. It was Switzerland advancing in group E with Brazil to get us the winnings for Switzerland and Serbia. It was the last day drama when Iran nearly knocked out Ronaldo's Portugal, ending in a 1-1 tie, and had Iran missing out on advancing while Spain just edged Portugal to win the group on 5 points because they had scored one more goal over the three games. It was the simple fact that all the games were close. There were two moments that really stood out though from match week 3. Each for different reasons.

One was a feel-good moment for our bets. I was huddled over my sushi bowl outside in humid Charlotte and fixated on my phone as I watched South Korea play Germany. South Korea had one thing to play for and that was pride. They had been eliminated after their second loss to Mexico and, meanwhile, Germany had everything to play for. If the Germans won they would advance and they could still advance with a tie as long as Mexico held off Sweden. While that was a position many teams would have taken coming into the tournament it was one that Germany did not expect to find itself in; they were the finely-tuned German machine after all and most recent World Champions. After their capitulation against Mexico and then a last second winner against Sweden they were fortunate to have a chance.

On matchday 3 both games from a given group have simultaneous kickoffs. While Mexico and Sweden were tied at the half Sweden started scoring in the second. Not one, not two, but three goals for the Swedes occurred in about a 25 minute window. Germany and South Korea still stood at 0-0. All of this was bad news for Germany. Now the Germans would have to win outright to advance. As it stood, with about 20 minutes in both games, Sweden and Mexico would advance both having 6 points and Germany would be on the outside looking in, sitting on 4. More importantly we would unbelievably win all of our bets from Group F, including that $60 bet on Germany not advancing at +1000.

It was balls to the wall time for the Die Mannschaft. Germany had to push for a goal and push they did. It was the only way out. The clock was not their friend and it kept ticking. Each minute the Germans were expending tremendous amounts of energy to get and retain the ball and push for a winner. In a sudden moment, in extra time, the camel's back broke.

Kim Young-gwon found himself inside the box, ball at his feet, and delivered the ball into the upper shelf of the goal. It was pandemonium. Germany had no chance and viewers around the world were shocked that the defending champions, like Italy and Spain in recent times, would once again not make it out of the group stage. In their last moments of desperation, the Germans moved their goalkeeper up the field for many of the set pieces and got caught out of position. They were doomed to a counter attack. 2-0. This is really happening and then the authoritative final whistle came. We would be collecting $2,845 on the Group F initial bet of $1,180. This would be able to at least subsidize some of the losses we were seeing in the other groups.

The other moment was memorable but not for a favorable result. In Group H Poland was in a similar position to South

Korea against Germany. Poland had been eliminated, after losing their first two games, and had just pride to play for. Poland's third opponent, Japan, had unexpectedly gotten a win over a 10 men Colombia team in the opener and a late equalizer against Senegal to be looking relatively good going into match three sitting on 4 points. If they got a tie they were through. It was a similar setup in the other game as Senegal, on 4 points, faced Colombia, on 3 points. Senegal just needed a tie to advance where as Colombia needed a win. While we greatly wanted Senegal to advance we were not so lucky but not for the reason I would have guessed.

What proceeded I remember having to look at like five different times to check. Poland won 1-0 against Japan and Colombia won 1-0 against Senegal. Colombia was through with 6 points but Japan and Senegal both had 4. Who gets to advance?

The tie breaking procedures were about to come into play in a way that had never been seen before in a World Cup. If tied on points we look at goal differential. They both were sitting on a 0-goal differential. We then look at goals scored. Both had scored four goals. How did they do head to head? Well they tied 2-2. At this point we are in unchartered territory. The next tie breaker is what they called the fair play points tiebreaker. It rewards the team with the lesser number of yellow and red cards through a point system. After two years of qualifying and then three hard fought matches this would be the decider.

Unfortunately for us Japan only had four yellow cards compared to Senegal's six through the three World Cup games. Senegal would be sent home. Japan would advance and complete our doomsday scenario of Colombia and Japan getting out of Group H. Falling on the wrong side of this tie breaker was about a $1,200 swing and would result in us losing our entire $1,460 of betting dollars for Group H. But as they say the ball is round... And in our case our bet was even rounder.

After the Group Stage

While the post group stage segment of the tournament became more and more fierce we had significantly less skin in the game. We only had four bets remaining: $10 bets on Switzerland and Portugal to win it all and $40 bets on Brazil and France to win it all. While just a week prior we were hoping Portugal would just lose to Iran we now found ourselves pulling for them in their matchup with Uruguay. It was short lived.

Portugal was eliminated. Then Switzerland lost out to Sweden. Our crop was diminishing fast. Brazil was eliminated in the next round to Belgium despite having the majority of possession and more shots. Our remaining money lay with France. We would collect $260 if France went on to win. They methodically won each game and finally found themselves in the final against Croatia. It seems the Soccernomics guys really were onto something when they analyzed countries and said that many of the former Yugoslavian countries outperform their resources. Croatia had officially arrived on the world stage.

The France bet, in comparison to many of the group stage bets, was not a lot of money and, I'm embarrassed to say, I found myself pulling for Croatia in the final. It is just human nature to pull for David and not Goliath, right? A couple questionable calls that lead to goals early on and next thing you know the complexion of the game has turned in favor of Goliath. This made it tough for Croatia to come back. The game ended 4-2 in a high scoring affair which contradicted the type of game we had come to know for most of the tournament. While emotionally I felt robbed there are many worse things than being able to go collect $260 for picking the right World Cup champion.

Final Thoughts (The Bet is Round)

We basically only won two of the eight groups, Group E and Group F, with a small consolation prize in picking the World Cup winner from Group C in France. After all was said and done we unfortunately lost about 27% of the $8,010 that we bet, about $1,600, of which about $1,200 was my own.

Writing this book has been incredibly helpful in analyzing my betting allocations. Like I had said very early on I was mostly looking at the individual bets but while in Dover I really started thinking about the group from a more holistic view and during this book writing I've really dialed in on the initial allocations. The next iteration of models I come up with will be able to show the return distributions for all the groups as I change the betting allocation. It may make sense in certain circumstances to place bets even when I think they may be a bit overpriced. It just depends what type of return distribution I am hoping for and how risky I feel.

When looking at all the charts it really did not make sense to bet so much on the Group H, the Poland and Japan nightmare group, when the distribution looked so similar to the Spain and Portugal group, a group which I bet very little on. Just because a bet looks overpriced in isolation does not mean that a collection of bets, including that overpriced bet, will look poor in aggregate and vice versa. This is one of my great take away's from this post World Cup analysis.

Were using FIFA rankings effective? While I wish they would have been more effective in our betting outcomes looking at the knock out stage teams by original pot speaks loudly. Only Germany and Poland from pot 1, the best teams and Russia, didn't get out of the group stage. Only Peru from pot 2 didn't make it out of the group stage. The weaker pots contributed many fewer teams to the knock out stage. Only Sweden and Denmark from pot 3 made it out of the group stage. And by the fair play tie breaker Japan was the only team from pot 4 to make it out of the group stage. To summarize 13 of the 16 knockout stage teams came from pot 1 or 2 which were supposed to be the strongest teams in their groups, according to their FIFA rankings.

I hope I inspire people interested in sports analytics to try their hand at some predictions. Maybe you will be the one that forms a comprehensive player database that is easy to pull from, that includes salaries going back 10 years. Maybe you can figure out some unorthodox metric that is useful when predicting the outcome of games.

While I did lose $1,200 of my own money the knowledge, satisfaction, fun, and maybe future earnings of this book made it well worth it. I will look back on these months as months well spent and will have very vivid memories to tell people in future years. And on a Thursday at trivia sometime in the future if the question is, "what was the only team to have been eliminated from a World Cup group stage because they had more yellow cards than the other team they were tied with?"

I will confidently, quickly, and, unfortunately, painfully be able to respond, "Senegal."

Appendix

By Pot

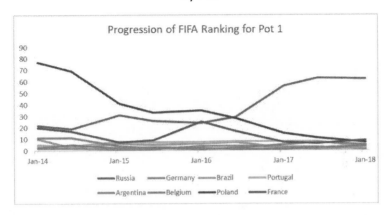

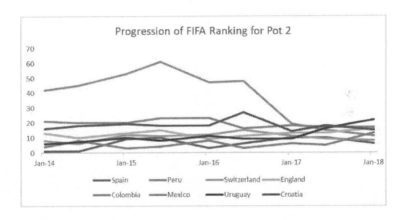

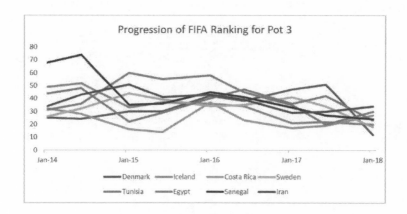

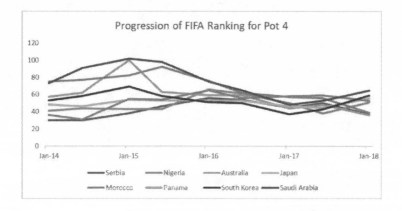

By Group

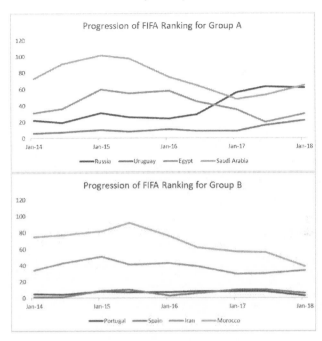

Progression of FIFA Ranking for Group A
— Russia — Uruguay — Egypt — Saudi Arabia

Progression of FIFA Ranking for Group B
— Portugal — Spain — Iran — Morocco

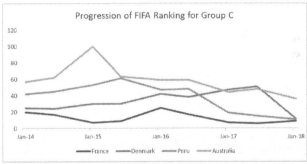

Progression of FIFA Ranking for Group C
— France — Denmark — Peru — Australia

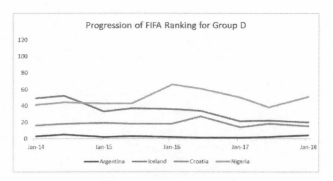

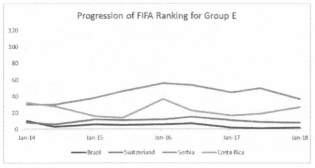

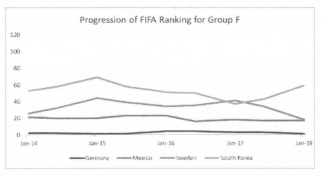

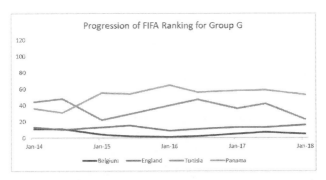

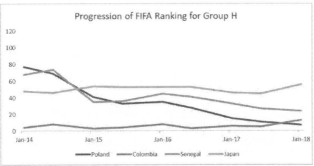

143

Readings Cited

1. Jacek Santorski, *Difficult Questions in Polish-Jewish Dialogue*
2. Simon Kuper and Stefan Szymanski, *Soccernomics*
3. Stefan Szymanski, *Money and Soccer*

Made in the USA
Columbia, SC
03 July 2021

41097501R00088